ARAB-TURKISH RELATIONS AND THE EMERGENCE OF ARAB NATIONALISM

by

ZEINE N. ZEINE, M.A., Ph.D. (Lond.)

Published by

K H A Y A T ' S

32 - 34 Rue Bliss
Beirut, Lebanon

CONTENTS

PREFACE

The purpose of this Essay is to set forth and reinterpret the Arab-Turkish relations in the nineteenth and the beginning of the twentieth centuries and to describe the emergence of Arab nationalism. Those relations constitute a most important background to some of the contemporary political problems in the Arab Near East and to the awakening of Arab political consciousness in this area. The work attempts also to remove certain fallacies and misconceptions concerning the relations between Arabs and Turks and the genesis of Arab nationalism.

The Arabs referred to in this Essay are primarily those Arabs who lived in the old geographic "Syria", i.e. the "Syrian Vilayet" of the Ottoman days where a very active intellectual and political opposition to Turkish rule was born towards the end of the nineteenth and the beginning of the twentieth centuries. It is hoped that these pages will provide some useful material for a more thorough and detailed study of the subject in the future when more documents, particularly from Turkish sources, may be available.

A "landmark" had to be chosen for the "beginning" of this work. I chose 1841, the year that saw the conclusion of the Treaty of London which conferred upon Muhammad 'Ali the Pashalik of Egypt in hereditary succession. It was also the year which marked the first phase of a series of active and even military interventions by the Great Powers in the Ottoman Empire, followed by its rapid decline and culminating in the catastrophe of the First World War, the destruction of that Empire and the birth of the modern Arab States.

I would like to express my deep gratitude for the help received from the following eminent Arab leaders—some of whom are no longer living—who shared with me their experiences and their intimate knowledge of the last years of the Turkish regime with which they were contemporary and of the birth of Arab independence in which several of them were directly concerned and played an important rôle: Faris Nimr Pasha, Faris el-Khuri, Shaikh 'Arif al-Zain, Tawfiq al-Natur, Sa'id Haidar, the Emir 'Adil Arslan, Sati' al-Husri and Shaikh 'Abdu'l Qadir al-Maghribi. I owe special thanks, also, to two eminent Turks, General 'Ali Fuad Pasha Cebesoy for his assistance in clarifying certain important issues with his first-hand knowledge of Arab-Turkish relations during the First World War and Professor Enver Ziya Karal, Professor of Modern History at the Faculty of Languages, History and Geography of Ankara University. Professor Karal kindly read the entire manuscript and I am deeply indebted to him for his valuable suggestions. Several friends and colleagues have also read either all or parts of the manuscript and I am very grateful to them for their kind advice and assistance. I would like to mention, in particular, Professor Albert Hourani, Professor Charles Issawi, Mr. 'Abdu'l Rahman 'Adra, Mr. Fuad Sarruf and Professors Leslie W. Leavitt, George Kirk, and Christopher H. O. Scaife. But in all fairness to them all, it must be stated that I hold myself responsible for the views and opinions expressed in this work.

One more word of acknowledgement: the opportunity for writing this book was provided by the Arab Studies Programme of the School of Arts and Sciences, under the directorship of Dr. Nabih A. Faris, at the American University of Beirut.

Zeine N. Zeine

American University of Beirut,
Beirut, Lebanon.
January 1958.

CHAPTER I

THE OTTOMANS AND THE OTTOMAN CONQUEST
OF THE NEAR EAST

The Turks are the third Islamic peoples of the Middle East, the first two being the Arabs and the Persians. But they established the largest and strongest Muslim Empire since the rise of Islam. At one time, the Turkish Empire stretched from the gates of Vienna to the straits of Bab-el-Mandib, and from the Caucasus to, almost, the Atlantic Ocean across North Africa. A series of decisive victories in a long chain of conquests led the Turks to the zenith of their military power and glory.[1] An unbroken succession of brilliant and great Sultans, the like of which has never been known in any other country, led the Ottomans to acquire in the fourteenth, fifteenth and sixteenth centuries a vast empire: Uthman ("Osman") at the time of whose death in 1326 the city of Brusa fell in Ottoman hands; Orkhan, the founder of the Janissaries (the Yeni-Cheri) and the conqueror of Nicomedia, Nicaea and Pergamum; Murad I, who crossed the Hellespont and won several victories in Europe, particularly at Adrianople in 1361 which henceforth became the capital of the Ottoman dominions and at Kossovo in 1389; Bayezid I was the great victor at the famous battle of Nicopolis (1396)[2] and the conqueror of Greece (Athens fell in 1397); Muhammad I, through his wisdom and courage reunited the Empire at the beginning of the fifteenth century when it seemed to have fallen into irretrievable ruin; Murad II won the decisive battle of Varna in 1444 against a Christian army which was "the most splendid that had been assembled since the French chivalry and the Hungarians advanced against Bajazet at Nicopolis";[3] Muhammad II, surnamed *Al-Fatih,* "the Conqueror", captured Constantinople in 1453 and made that city "the centre jewel in the ring of the Turkish

Empire"; Selim I led his victorious army southwards and in less than two years added Syria, Egypt and Arabia (1516-1517) to the Ottoman dominions and finally Sultan Sulaiman, "the Magnificent", "the Law-Giver", "the Lord of his Age", "the Perfecter of the Perfect Number",[4] captured Belgrade, invaded Hungary and won the decisive battle of Mohacz (1526), occupied Budapest, besieged Vienna (1529) and added Mosul and Baghdad (1535) to the Ottoman Empire. In his time, the Turkish dominions formed "an empire embracing many of the richest and most beautiful regions of the world...and which under no subsequent Sultan maintained or recovered the wealth, power and prosperity which it enjoyed under the great lawgiver of the House of Othman."[5] No wonder then if Richard Knolles wrote: "...At this present if you consider the beginning, progress and perpetual felicity of this the Ottoman Empire, there is in this world nothing more admirable and strange; if the greatness and lustre thereof, nothing more magnificent and glorious; if the Power and Strength thereof, nothing more Dreadful and Dangerous, which...holdeth all the world in scorn thundering out nothing but Blood and War, with a full persuasion in time to Rule over all, prefixing unto itself no other limits than the uttermost bounds of the Earth, from the rising of the Sun unto the going down of the same."[6]

The origin of the Turks who established such an empire, their arrival from central Asia in Anatolia in the middle of the thirteenth century and their employment by the Seljuk Sultans, are all wrapped in legend and obscurity.[7] We know that Osman (1288-1326) or Uthman, son of Ertoghrul, was the founder of the Turkish dynasty which gave the name Ottoman[8] to the Empire that it established and which lasted for nearly six hundred years, under thirty-seven Sultans. But we do not know much more about him. This Empire, however, could not have been the work of a group of adventurers or a band of nomads "flying from the highlands of Central Asia before the fierce onset of the Mongols". F. Köprülü criticises H. A. Gibbons for accepting the legendary history of the Ottomans in his work, *The Foundation of the Ottoman Empire,* and believes that it is a mistake to attribute the establishment of this Empire to the Muslim zeal and enthusiasm of a tribe of 400 tents which settled in the thirteenth century in the north-west corner of Anatolia. He is of the opinion that in the first half of the fourteenth century, the Seljukid Empire had reached its political and cultural climax, and had already one of the most advanced economic and social organizations of the Middle Ages. The Ottoman Empire grew out of the political and social synthesis of all the Turkish elements in Anatolia during the thirteenth and fourteenth centuries.[9]

As to the Islamization of the Ottomans, there seems to be little agreement among historians concerning the time and circumstances which made the Ottoman Turks adopt Islam. Gibbons says that there is no historical evidence that the tribe to which Uthman belonged was Muslim. These new arrivals in Anatolia became Muslim in the thirteenth century only after settling among the Seljuk Turks, who were already Muslims. Köprülü thinks that it is unwise to conclude from legends that Uthman was converted to Islam. He dismisses the question of the Islamization of the Ottomans by saying.: "These Turkish tribes were in general Muslims but free from all fanaticism. The precepts of religion were too complicated and impossible for them to observe, so they remained faithful to their national traditions, covered with a light varnish of Islamism..."[10] It is believed that Islam first penetrated among the Turkish tribes in Transoxiana sometime, approximately, between the years 820 and 1000[11] when the Arabs first came in contact with the Turks. Al-Mansur, the second Abbasid Caliph (754-775), was the first Caliph to have a small corps of Turkish soldiers in his army. Moreover, as a result of the Muslim wars in Turkestan, such cities as Bokhara, Samarkand, Farghanah and Ashrusnah were in the habit of sending "as part of the poll-tax" children of the nomads of Turkestan, ordinarily taken captives and so made slaves, according to the custom of those days. But it was actually during the reign of Al-Mu'tasim (833-842), the third son of Harun-al-Rashid, that large numbers of Turks entered into the household of a Caliph.[12] Afraid of the Persians who had become so influential in the days of his brother Amin, and having no confidence in the Arabs "whose chauvinism had departed, and who, spoiled by the luxury of town life, had lost their vigour", he turned towards the Turks to gain their support and protection, his own mother being one of them. In the thirteenth century, large numbers of Turks entered the Muslim Empire, especially into Persia, Iraq and Syria in the days of the great Turkish dynasty of the Seljukids. But it remained for the Ottomans to be the first Turks to conquer the Arab lands of the Near East from the Mamluks of Egypt who, then, ruled those lands.

At the beginning of the sixteenth century, the three Powers which ruled the Middle East were the Ottomans, the Persians and the Mamluk sultans of Egypt and Syria. Persia's power was expanding under the Safawid ruler, Shah Isma'il. The Mamluks, on the other hand, weakened in war, particularly against the Mongols, had lost their vigour and their army was inferior to the Ottomans in equipment and discipline. With the coming of *Yawuz* Sultan Selim—the Stern and Inflexible—to the throne, the balance of power in the Middle East turned in favour of the Ottomans. In addition to various political and territorial reasons which had caused several wars between the Persians and the Turks, there was the old religious conflict between Shi'ism and Sunnism. Persia was a Shi'ite country, and Shah Isma'il, who supported a vigorous Shi'ite policy, had made Shi'ism the state religion. He had also made a treaty with the Mamluks in 1514 as a result of which the latter had broken their diplomatic relations with Sultan Selim. Sultan Selim, on the other hand, considered himself as the champion and protector of Sunnism and had massacred thousands of Shi'ites in his domains. In 1514, Sultan Selim undertook a new campaign against Persia and defeated Shah Isma'il's army on the plain of Chalderan, between lake Urmia and Tabriz. As a result of this victory, Eastern Anatolia and Upper Mesopotamia, including Kurdistan, were added to the Turkish Empire.

The next concern of Sultan Selim was to get rid of the power of the Mamluks who had made a treaty with Shah Isma'il and broken their diplomatic relations with the Ottoman Government. At the head of a large army, Selim advanced towards Syria in the latter part of 1516. But, meanwhile, the Mamluk Sultan Qansaw al-Ghawri had left Cairo with a strong army and moved to the north of Syria. On August 24, 1516, the two armies clashed on the plain of Marj Dabiq, north of Aleppo. The Mamluk forces were decisively defeated by the Ottoman army. The battle lasted only a few hours—from sunrise till late afternoon. The Sultan himself was killed. His cavalry was thrown into disorder by the gunfire of the Turks and fled in panic. Hama fell on September 20, Homs on the 22nd, Damascus on October 9. Nearly four months later, on January 22, 1517, having crossed the Sinai desert on their way to Cairo, the Ottoman troops fought and won the decisive battle of Raydaniyah. Ten days later, Cairo was in Ottoman hands and on April 17, Tuman-Bay, the last of the Mamluk Sultans, perished at the hands of Sultan Selim's executioners. Egypt became a part of the Ottoman Empire and that extraordinary dynasty of Mamluks or slave kings, which had ruled Egypt and the Arab lands in the Near East from 1250 came to an end. "Thus", wrote Ibn Iyas, "the rule of al-Ashraf al-Ghawri came to an end, in the twinkling of an eye, as though he had never been. Praise be to Him whose Kingdom never wanes, and who never changes! Thus he and his kingdom came to an end together; the kingdom of Egypt and the Dominion of Syria, over which he had reigned for fifteen years, nine months and twenty days..."[13]

In the absence of any new evidence, it seems that the Arab lands which were conquered from the Mamluks by Sultan Selim were not directly administered from Constantinople, as is shown "from a study of the bureaus, and from the separate listing of the revenues from Syria, Mesopotamia, and Egypt in contemporary estimates."[14] Moreover, Arabia, the cradle of Islam, was hardly ever under the direct or rigid control of the Ottomans. "The Holy Cities of Mecca and Medina, far from paying tribute, received a large annual subsidy at the cost of Egypt."[15] Indeed, the Arabic-speaking provinces were "regarded by the Ottoman ruling class, at least in the beginning, with a certain deference which they did not accord to the rest of the Sultan's dominions—for the very reason that its inhabitants did speak the sacred language, while most of them at the same time professed the dominant religion".[16]

Almost complete local and internal independence was left to the feudal Emirs and the local chiefs in Arab lands, particularly in Lebanon. After the conquest of Egypt, Sultan Selim returned to Damascus and sonfirmed in office Al-Ghazali as the *Vali* of

Syria, annexing to that *Vilayet* Jerusalem, Gaza, Safad and Al-Karak. In "Southern Syria", i.e. Lebanon, all the feudal lords paid homage to him except the Tanukhi emirs who refused to appear before him, having remained faithful to the Mamluks when the latter fought against Sultan Selim at Marj Dabiq. He was much impressed by the dignity and personality of Emir Fakhr-al-Din whose title in those days was *Sultan al-Barr* (the king of the land) and *Emir Lubnan*. Selim confirmed him in office as the Emir of the district of Shuf. Other principal Emirs who were confirmed in their fiefdoms were Emir 'Assaf Mansur al-Turkumani in Kisrawan and Jubail and the Banu Sifas in 'Akkar and Tripoli.[17] The remaining lands were, in the same way, left to their feudal lords. Sultan Selim also appointed governors for Aleppo, Homs, Tripoli and other coastal towns. "The keynote of Ottoman administration" wrote Gibb and Bowen, "was conservatism, and all the institutions of government were directed to the maintenance of the status quo."[18] But the keeping of the status-quo meant also the keeping of all the internal troubles and feuds among the Emirs owing to their rivalries and jealousies, leading to rebellions and internecine wars. The Ottoman Sultan asserted his authority in the last resort by armed intervention.[19] The system of local feudal government in Syria and Lebanon, superimposed by a loose Turkish administration headed by a Turkish Governor General and supported by a Turkish army, continued down to the latter part of the nineteenth century.

It is not possible to know for certain what the Arab-Turkish relations were in the early days of Ottoman rule. But all the generalisations and sweeping statements made during the second half of the nineteenth and the beginning of the twentieth centuries about the antipathy between those two races, such as: "the Arab hated and mistrusted the Turk, the Turk hated and mistrusted the Arab", are grossly exaggerated and certainly do not apply to the early centuries of Ottoman administration. In their Introduction to *Islamic Society and the West,* H.A.R. Gibb and Harold Bowen have made an important contribution to the study of Turkish history when they say: "Current views on Turkey and Egypt in the eighteenth century so abound with misconceptions, which we ourselves shared at the outset of our study, that it is our first duty to marshal for others the data which have led us to very different conclusions". The Turks made no attempt to assimilate the non-Turkish elements in their Empire and the Arabs were the largest of these elements.[20] Indeed, in the Arab provinces of their Empire, the Turks remained "strangers". No large bodies of them settled in those lands. As a ruling class, they sent their government officials and their soldiers but not for long, as the Turkish officials were continuously changed. As G. W. F. Stripling has pointed out: "The Mamelukes, after all, had practically been brought up in Syria and Egypt, and consequently they had some interest in the appearance and reputation of their home. The Turks, however, were sent for a term, none too long to familiarize themselves with the conditions of their charges, and very frequently, after a brief sojourn amongst the Arabs, they returned to Turkey for the rest of their lives, or were assigned to some other posts remote from the Arabs, or at best in other parts of the Arab lands where conditions were quite different from those with which they were familiar....Assimilation could not take place under such conditions."[21]

But there are a number of important points to remember in connection with the relations between Arabs and Turks. The Ottomans did not conquer the Arab lands from the Arabs. They fought the Mamluks, not the Arabs. Indeed, there is no evidence that, at first, the Arabs took much interest in their new masters. The Arab fortunes as well as the institution of the Caliphate had long passed their lowest ebb as a result of a long period of decay and disintegration which had set in since the tenth century. "The line of 'Abbasid Caliphs in Cairo were mere court functionaries of the Mamluk Sultans. The Egyptian historian Maqrizi (d. 1442) remarks: 'The Turkish Mamluks installed as Caliph a man to whom they gave the name and titles of Caliph. He had no authority and no right to express his opinion. He passed his time with the commanders, the great officers, the officials and the judges, visiting them to thank them for the dinners and parties to which they had invited him."[22] It is safe to say that Ottoman rule protected the Arab world and Islam from foreign encroachments for nearly four hundred years and in general accorded a wide measure of local autonomy to the Arab provinces, except during the last

years of 'Abdu'l Hamid's despotic and corrupt administration
and the brief period of the Young Turks' Turanian chauvinism.
Although Turkish was the official language of administration and
government and the majority of the Turks never learned Arabic,
yet not only many Arabic words found their way into their language but prayers and readings from the Qur'an in the mosques
of Constantinople and other Turkish towns were always in Arabic.
The Arabs were proud that the Arabic language—their most cherished and precious heritage, after Islam—remained the spiritual
language of the Turks.

The Muslim Arabs played, also, an important rôle in the
Judicial system of the Ottoman Empire and thus wielded much
power in the internal administration of that Empire. Indeed, the
backbone of Ottoman Government—the Muslim Sacred *Shari'ah*—
could not be maintained without a knowledge of the Arabic
language. After all, the Qur'an and all other sources of Muslim
Jurisprudence were all in Arabic. The University of Al-Azhar in
Cairo and the Sunni religious schools of Damascus, Tripoli and
Aleppo trained a large number of 'Ulamas, Qadis and Muftis well
versed in Muslim law and jurisprudence. They were appointed to
various religious courts throughout the Empire and thus occupied
positions of great influence and importance.[23] As to the *Shaikh-
al-Islam*, he was the head of the Muslim legislature and the authoritative exponent of the Sacred Law. It seems that the title
originated with Muhammad II, the *Shaikh-al-Islam* being originally the Grand Mufti of Constantinople. "He is the authorized
interpreter of the Kuran and, strictly speaking, no legislative or
executive act can be valid without his sanction pronounced by
an authoritative decree (fetva) declaring that it is in conformity
with the Sacred Law."[24] The importance of his office was so great
that he could demand the obedience of even the Sultan himself.
Indeed, to remove a Sultan from the throne, the sanction of
Shaikh-al-Islam in the form of a *"fatwa"* was necessary in order
to at least "legalize" that action in the eyes of the Muslims. Such
a *"fatwa"* was issued when the following Sultans were deposed:
Selim III (1808), 'Abdu'l 'Aziz (1876), Murad V (1876) and
'Abdu'l Hamid II (1909). The *Shaikh-al-Islam* was appointed by

the Sultan himself and resided in Constantinople. He and the Grand Vizier were the two highest and most influential officials of the Empire.

Thus, the most important factor which bound the Arabs to the Turks and made the former acquiesce in the rule of their nationally alien Turkish masters, was Islam. This is the cardinal element in Arab-Turkish relations for nearly four centuries. The Ottoman Turks were Muslims, and the Ottoman Sultans were *Ghâzîs,* i.e. the champions of Islam, the " warriors of the Faith", the "Sword of God" and the "protector and the refuge of the believers".[25] The Arab lands found themselves part of the most powerful Muslim Empire that had existed since the rise of Islam. Although the circumstances which led the last puppet Caliph under the Mamluks in Egypt, Al-Mutawakkil, to transfer—if there was a transfer—the office of the Caliphate to Sultan Selim, are obscure and are not discussed by any contemporary historian,[26] the fact remains that for four hundred years the Ottoman Sultans fell heir to the institution of the Caliphate.[27] Following the tradition of their predecessors, they also became the "Protectors" of the twin Holy Cities of Mecca and Medina in Arabia, assuming the title of *Khadim al-Haramain al-Sharifain,* after Sultan Selim had received from Sayyid Barakat, the Sharif of Mecca, the keys of that city as a symbol of obedience and loyalty. Consequently, up until the beginning of the twentieth century when the Arabs became politically nation-conscious, the fact that the Ottoman Empire was "Turkish" did not matter so much as the fact that it was Muslim. The Turks and the vast majority of the Arabs were members of one great *Muslim* Community united by their faith and their allegiance to a Muslim sovereign—the Padishah-Caliph—who was "the Vicar of God on earth", "the Successor of the Prophet", *Imam-al-Muslimin,* the Pontiff of Muslims, "'Alam Panah", the Refuge of the world, *Zill-Allah,* the Shadow of God, and *Khadim al-Haramain al-Sharifain,* the Servant of the two Holy Sanctuaries.'[28] The capital of their Empire, Constantinople, had been renamed "Islambul" (later corrupted to Istanbul) i.e. the city where "Islam abounds".[29] Moreover, in the minds of the European writers on the Ottoman Empire, the word

Turk included all the Muslim inhabitants of that Empire, regardless of their race or nationality.[30] The word "Arab" was specifically reserved for Bedouins and the nomads of the desert.

It is not true to say that the Arabs were for four hundred years powerless under the Turks, nor that the Arab lands were depleted and despoiled by Turkish occupation. Nor is it true to say that the Muslim Arabs were not allowed to bear arms or serve in the Ottoman armies. High Arab army officers and Arab troops have distinguished themselves in the Turkish armies.[31] Many Arabs served in very important and influential positions in the Ottoman Empire but it will not be possible to compile a full list of them because often both their religion and their Turkish education identified them so thoroughly with the Turks. General Nuri Pasha al-Sa'id, several times Prime Minister in modern Iraq and who had served in the Turkish army during the first World War, has written: "In the Ottoman Empire, Arabs, as Muslims, were regarded as partners of the Turks. They shared with the Turks both rights and responsibilities, without any racial distinction: the higher appointments in the State, whether military or civil, were open to the Arabs; they were represented in both the upper and the lower houses of the Ottoman Parliament. Many Arabs became Prime Ministers, *Shaikh al-Islam*, Generals and Walis, and Arabs were always to be found in all ranks of the State services."[32]

There is no historical evidence to support the popular view current in the twentieth century that the Turks were mainly responsible for Arab "backwardness" and cultural retardation for four hundred years. On the contrary, the Arab lands seem to have profited from the Turkish occupation. "Syria", Gibb and Bowen have written, "had probably benefited materially more than any other Asiatic province from incorporation in the Ottoman Empire, as a result of the commercial connexions thus formed and enjoyed a fairly flourishing social and economic life."[33] It may well be that the Arabs, up to the reign of 'Abdu'l Hamid, suffered not from too much Turkish Government but actually from too little of it! It must also be said in all fairness that the Turks did not attempt to assimilate or Turkify the Arabs until the coming to power of the Committee of Union and Progress in 1908. Generally speaking, up until the end of the nineteenth century, the Arabs seem to have suffered more from their own feudal lords, their feuds and rivalries and their conflicts with the Pashas, than from the central authority at Constantinople. Their internal dissensions, their tribal organizations and feudal institutions, their dynastic rivalries and their extreme individualism continued to keep them divided and weak. Moreover, the Muslim Arabs' belief in the perfection of the religious principles underlying their political and social institutions and in the sacredness of their language, as well as the memory of their "glorious past" and of their military conquests in the early days of Islam, had developed in them a feeling of "Arab" superiority. This "superiority complex" rendered them aloof and therefore unwilling to change their way of life for what they considered to be new-fangled and heretical ways introduced by the West, a West which to them was part of the Dar-al-Harb or the House of War.[34]

In the words of Professor Bernard Lewis:

"From its foundation until its fall, the Ottoman Empire was a state dedicated to the advancement or defence of the power and faith of Islam. For six centuries the Ottomans were almost constantly at war with the Christian West, first in the attempt—mainly successful—to impose Islamic rule on a large part of Europe, then in the long drawn out rearguard action to halt or delay the relentless counter-attack of the West... For the Ottoman, his Empire was Islam itself. In the Ottoman chronicles, the territories of the Empire are referred to as 'the lands of Islam', its armies as the 'soldiers of Islam', its religious head as 'the Sheikh of Islam'. Its people thought of themselves first and foremost as Muslims. 'Ottoman' was a dynastic name like Umayyad or Abbasid, which only acquired a national significance in the nineteenth century under the influence of European liberalism..."[35]

NOTES
AND REFERENCES

1. « ... l'Empire ottoman est resté durant tout le XVIème siècle et le XVIIème siècle une des plus grandes puissances du monde occidental, sinon la plus grande de toutes. Règnant sur plusieurs millions de kilomètres carrés, disposant de ressources budgetaires plus stables et plus larges que n'importe quel Etat européen (y compris l'Espagne et ses mines d'or), servis par une administration méthodiquement organisée et devouée au bien public, sûrs de la fidelité d'un people chez lequel la discipline compte au premier rang des vertus tradition-nelles, ayant les meilleures troupes régulières, la meilleure artillerie, une marine qui dominait toute la Méditerranée, les sultans obligeaient alors l'Europe entière à compter avec eux : Louis XIV, rappelait ré-cement F. Grenard d'une manière très opportune, si arrogant à faire respecter du Saint-Père des privilèges contestables, souffrait que son ambassadeur à Constantinople fut batonné et emprisonné, et tous les voyageurs européens au Levant étaient alors pénétrés, devant le spectacle de Stamboul, de cette admiration respectueuse qu'inspirent les grands foyers de civilisation. » Sauvaget, J., *Introduction à l'Histoire de l'Orient Musulman,* pp. 164-165.

2. After the battle of Nicopolis, Sultan Bayezid sent to the Mamluk Sultan of Egypt (Zahir Saif-ud-Din Barquq) a number of the heavily armed prisoners which his army had captured and they were paraded in the streets of Cairo. Then again, after the battle of Varna, Sultan Murad II sent some Hungarian prisoners this time to the Sultan of Herat in Afghanistan! The Sultan kept them and used them in his army as a "tank division". These giant warriors of the North must have produced a great impression in Egypt, in Afghanistan and in the Muslim world in general as the Ottomans were considered the champions of Islam. (From a Lecture on the Ottoman Empire by Professor Paul Wittek, delivered at the School of Oriental and African Studies, University of London, on March 8, 1951).

3. Creasy, Edward S., *History of the Ottoman Turks,* p. 64. "One hun-dred thousand paladins, the flower of the chivalry of France and Germany, nobles not a few from England, Scotland, Flanders, and Lombardy, and a large body of the Knights of St. John responded to the Papal call, and enlisted under the banner of Sigismund. In the battle of Nicopolis (1396) the forces of Christendom were overthrown by the Ottomans...The triumph of the Ottomans was complete." Mar-riott, J.A.R., *The Eastern Question* (Oxford 1917...1947), p. 66.

4. "Solayman was the tenth Sultan of the House of Othman; he opened the tenth century of the Hegira; and for these and other decimal attributes he was styled by his countrymen the Perfector of the Perfect Number". — Creasy, p. 160.

5. *Ibid*, p. 197.
Hammer, J. De, *Histoire de l'Empire Ottoman* (Transl.), (Paris, 1835), pp. 1-11; 55-75.

6. Knolles, Richard and Rycaut, Paul, *The Turkish History, From the Original of that Nation to the Growth of the Ottoman* Empire... Preface—"The Author to the Reader"—6th Edition, (London, 1687).

7. See Gibbons, H.A., *The Foundation of the Ottoman Empire* (Oxford, 1916); Barthold, V. V., *Histoire des Turcs d'Asie Centrale* (Adaptation Française par Mme M. Donskis), (Paris, 1945); Köprülü, M.F., *Les Origines de l'Empire Ottoman* (Paris, 1935); Wittek, P., *The Rise of the Ottoman Empire* (London, 1938).

8. The current usage of the word "Turk" appeared at the end of the Ottoman Empire. Originally, it was used to denote Anatolian peasants (corresponding to the word "Fellah" in Arabic). To call an Istanbul gentleman a Turk was an insult. He was a member of the Ottoman Empire.

9. Köprülü, pp. 29, 33, and 78.

10. *Ibid.*, p. 58.

11. Barthold, p. 47.

12. Muir, Sir William, *The Caliphate, Its Rise, Decline and Fall.* (London, 1899) pp. 437, 515-520;
Diehl, Charles et Marçais, Georges, *Histoire Générale*, vol. III : *Le Monde Oriental de 395 à 1081* (Paris, 1944), pp. 378-379, 572-573.

13. Ibn Iyas, *Bada'i' al-Zuhur fi Waqa'i' al-Duhur,* vol. III, (Cairo A.H. 1312) pp. 58 and 68.
For an account of the Ottoman conquest of Syria and Egypt see Salmon, W.H., *An Account of the Ottoman Conquest of Egypt in the Year A.H. 922* (A.D. 1516) (London, 1921) and Stripling, George W.F., *The Ottoman Turks and the Arabs, 1511-1574,* pp. 43-58. See, also, Toynbee, A.J., *A. Study of History,* vol. I, pp. 347-388.

14. Lybyer, E.H., *The Government of the Ottoman Empire in the Time of Suleiman the Magnificent,* p. 173.

15. Lybyer, p. 30. "Parts of the mountain lands of Albania and Kurdistan, and the desert of Arabia, though nominally under direct administration, were in very slight obedience; they retained their ancient tribal organizations, under hereditary chieftains who were invested with Ottoman titles in return for military service, and whose followers might or might not submit to taxation."—*Ibid*.

16. Gibb, H.A.R. and Bowen, H., *Islamic Society and the West,* p. 160.

17. See Al-Duwaihi, Mar Istefan, *Ta'rikh al-Taifah Al-Maruniyah* (Beirut, 1890), pp. 152-153, and *Ta'rikh al-Amir Haidar Ahmad Shihab* (Cairo, 1900), vol. I, pp. 561-562. See also Hitti, Philip K., *Lebanon in History* (London, 1957), pp. 357-359.

18. Gibb and Bowen, p. 200.
    « Enfin, il faut noter ce fait qu'il est exceptionel de voir les Ottomans imposer à une nouvelle province incorporée dans leur Empire, les lois, decréts ou règlements purement Ottomans ; au contraire, ils s'attachent toujours à maintenir en place les institutions anciennement établies, afin d'éviter de troubler la structure économique, sinon sociale du pays — la domination militaire et politique étant assurée. »
    — Mantran, Robert et Sauvaget, Jean, *Règlements Fiscaux Ottomans — Les Provinces Syriennes* (Beyrouth, 1951) Introduction, p. X.

19. "Conquered in the sixteenth century, the Arab lands had lapsed again to virtual independence of an anarchic sort before the seventeenth century was over ; and, indeed, over most of the Asiatic part of his Empire the Ottoman Sultan had come by then to exercise little better than an otiose suzerainty." Great Britain, *Handbooks prepared under the Direction of the Historical Section of the Foreign Office*, No. 88, *Turkey in Asia*, pp. 3-4.

20. See the statistics of population in Appendix A.

21. Stripling, p. 59.

22. Cited by Lewis, Bernard, in *The Arabs in History* (London, 1950), p. 155.

23. "The task of maintaining intact the traditions of the Mahommedan faith, and of insuring their observance by the successors of the Prophet, devolves upon the 'Ulemas', the Moslem doctors-in-law, whose functions are sacerdotal, juridical, and scholastic, and from whose ranks the Mullahs, the Imams and the Judges of the Cheri Courts are recruited."
    Gooch, G.P. and Temperley, Harold, *British Documents on the Origins of the War, 1898-1914*, vol. V, p. 6.

24. *Ibid.*, p. 6. See also Young, George, *Corps de Droit Ottoman*, vol. I, p. 6.
    "He had the right to appoint and promote all the other muftis of the empire, and in later times he appointed the qadis also ; his department included the *Fatwa-Khanah*, a bureau for the promulgation of formal legal decisions, either on matters of State, such as the declaration of war or peace, the validity of a proposed legislative enactment &c., or on matters of personal law, concerning private individuals."—Great Britain, *Handbooks Prepared Under the Direction of the Historical Section of the Foreign Office*—No. 96a & b, *The Rise of Islam and the Caliphate* (And) *The Pan-Islamic Movement*, p. 31.
    The sultans considered all their wars with the Christian powers in Europe as Holy Wars but the *Shaikh-al-Islam* alone had the right to declare a Holy War.

25. Wittek, pp. 14, 18, and 45.

26. "The popular account at the present day of the relations between Sultan Selim and the Khalifah Mutawakkil is that the Caliph made a formal transfer of his office to the conqueror, and as a symbol of this transference handed over to him the sacred relics, which were believed to have come down from the days of the Prophet—the robe, of which mention has already been made as being worn by the Abbasids of Baghdad on solemn state occasions—some hairs from his beard, and the sword of the Caliph 'Umar. There is no doubt that Selim carried off these reputed relics to Constantinople (where they are still preserved in the mosque of Ayyub), as part of the loot which he acquired by the conquest of Egypt; but of the alleged transfer of the dignity of the Khilafat there is no contemporary evidence at all." Arnold, Sir Thomas W., *The Caliphate* (London, 1924), pp. 142-143.

27. "As the claim to the Caliphate on the ground of descent from the Quraish was, in the case of an Ottoman Sultan, impossible, his assumption of the title was defended by complaisant jurists on the ground that the Moslems must have an *imam*, and that the office must be in the hands of a sovereign powerful enough to exercise the functions proper to it—the defence of religion and the government of the state—in accordance with Qur'an IV, 62: 'Obey God and the Prophet and those who have rule over you'. The theological and legal defence for the Caliphate being in the possession of the Sultans of Turkey was based on the following considerations: (1) the possession of power, (2) election, (3) nomination by the last Abbasaid Caliph, (4) guardianship of the Holy Cities, and (5) possession of the relics of the Prophet." *Handbooks Prepared under the Direction of the Historical Section of the Foreign Office, No. 96a & b., The Rise of Islam and the Caliphate — The Pan-Islamic Movement,* pp. 43-44.

    The opening line of a *Fatwa* issued by Shaikh al-Islam 'Abdu'l Rahim Effendi during the reign of Sultan Ahmad III (1703-1730) begins thus: *"Padishah-i-Islam* whose Caliphate will endure until the Day of Judgment...". See Document XXII in *Topkapi Sarayi Müzessi Arsivi Kilavuzu,* vol. II (Istanbul, 1940).

28. "When a new Sultan was proclaimed to be the ruler of the Ottoman Empire, he was girt with the sword of Osman, the founder of the dynasty. The ceremony corresponding to the Coronation of Christian Kings in Europe, took place in the Mosque of Eyyub, situated at the end of the Golden Horn, outside the walls of Constantinople. It was traditionally performed by the Head of the Mowlawi Derwishes, called Chelebi Effendi".—Pears, Sir Edwin, *Forty Years in Constantinople,* p. 176.

    In the capitulations granted to England in 1675, Sultan Muhammad IV spoke of himself as: "Moy qui suis le puissant Seigneur des Seigneurs du monde, dont le nom est formidable sure Terre, Distributeur de toutes les couronnes de l'Univers, Sultan Mahomet Han... Cette Haute Porte Impériale qui est le réfuge des Princes du monde, et la retraite des Rois de tout l'Univers."—Hinckley, Frank E., *American Consular Jurisdiction in the Orient* (Washington, D.C. 1906), p. 7.

29. There are numerous evidences in Istanbul today that not long ago Islam did abound in it, that Turkey was indeed a *Muslim* country. To give only one example: when the visitor enters the famous Seraglio by the Babi Humayun (the Imperial Gate) and passes through the Court of the Janissaries he finds at the end of the Court the Orta Kapi (the Middle Gate) which leads into the inner Court of the Serai. On top of the Orta Kapi, in large and imposing letters, there is the following inscription *in Arabic:* "There is no god but God, and Muhammad is The Messenger of God."

30. Rev. William Jowett, author of *Christian Researches in the Mediterranean* (London, 1822), p. 421, quotes a letter from Rev. James Connor, dated February 23, 1820, who writes: "Our Consul told me that the population of Beirut amounts to about 10,000 souls. Of these about 3,000 are Turks and the remainder Christians of various denominations". The word "Turk" here obviously stands for Muslim and therefore Arab. Very few Turks ever inhabited the Arab provinces of their Empire.

31. To mention only some outstanding examples: General 'Ali Fuad Pasha Cebesoy told the author that Arab troops from the regions of Damascus, Aleppo and Jerusalem distinguished themselves highly under Osman Pasha at Plevna, between July and December 1877 and again in 1915 at Gallipoli and in 1916 in Rumania, at the Battle of Argostoli.

32. As-Sa'id, General Nuri, *Arab Independence and Unity* (Baghdad, Government Press, 1943) p. 2.

33. Gibb and Bowen, vol. I, p. 218 ; Duwaihi, p. 153.

34. According to Muslims, the world is divided into two Houses or Domains, the House of War (Dar-al-Harb) inhabited by non-Muslims, and the House of Peace (Dar-al-Salam) inhabited by Muslims or true-believers. (One of the duties of true believers is to enlarge the latter at the expense of the former.)

35. See article on "Islamic Revival in Turkey" in *International Affairs,* vol. XXVIII, No. 1, January 1952, p. 47. (Published by the Royal Institute of International Affairs, London.)

CHAPTER II

OTTOMAN GOVERNMENT IN ARAB LANDS

The Ottoman Administrative system which borrowed its fundamental lines from Persian, Seljuk and Mamluk administrations resembled a pyramid at the top of which stood the smallest unit, the village[1] and the broad base of which rested on the *eyalet*. A number of villages formed a *Nahiyah* under a Mudir and a number of *Nahiyas* constituted a *Kaza* (Arabic *Qada*) ruled over by a Qa'im-Maqam (or Lieutenant-governor). Below the *Kazas* came the *sanjaks* (or liwas), each governed by a Mutasarrif. The *eyalet*, known also as *vilayet* (from the two Arabic words "iyalah" and "wilayah") was administered by a "Wali" *(Vali)* or Pasha. The *Vali* was the supreme governor-general of the province and had wide judicial powers. He "united in himself the supreme military and civil authority, and was responsible for public order and security, for the collection of taxes and the remittance of the stipulated annual tribute or contribution to Istanbul and for the public administration generally."[2] Although the Ottoman Empire was right from the beginning divided into *eyalets* and *sanjaks,* it was not until the reforms (the *Tanzimat*) of the nineteenth century, particularly the Hatti-Humayun of 1856, that the administrative units were reorganized, principally on the basis of Midhat Pasha's system introduced successfully in the *vilayet* of the Danube when he was its Pasha. Midhat Pasha had actually borrowed with slight modification the French administrative units based on geographic lines. The *vilayet* was the French *Department;* the *sanjak, l'Arrondissement;* the *Kaza,* le *Canton;* and the *nahiyas,* la *Commune.* Midhat Pasha's reforms were incorporated in "the laws of the *vilayets"* of 1864 and 1871.[3]

The elaborate system of government which operated in the Ottoman Empire was based on Muslim principles embodied in the

Shari'a, the Canon Law or the Sacred Law of Islam, administered by religious courts under the supreme authority of *Shaikh-al-Islam.* The supreme legislator *(Shâr'i')* in Muslim society is God Himself. He revealed His laws directly to the Prophet who transmitted them to mankind, first through the *Qur'an* and secondly, through his customary conduct and practices—the *Sunnah.* Hence *Shari'a* law is "sacred, infallible and immutable" and the Muslim government is the direct government of God. It is the supreme religious and social duty of every Muslim to submit to this Law before which all Muslims are equal. "The principle of unity and order which in other societies is called *civitas, polis,* State, in Islam is personified by Allah: Allah is the name of the supreme power acting in the common interest. Thus the public treasury is 'the treasury of Allah', the army is the army of Allah, even the public functionaries are 'the employees of Allah' ".[4]

Nearly three hundred years after the death of the Prophet, four schools of the interpretation of Tradition and *Qur'an* became well established. The interpreters were four great Muslim jurists and Imams whose teachings and legal explanations became the basis of the understanding and application of the *Shari'a* Law in different parts of the Muslim world. These four schools bear the names of their founders. They are the Hanafi, the Shâfi'i, the Hanbali and the Mâliki schools. When the *Shari'a,* became the fundamental law of the Ottoman Empire, the Ottomans officially adopted its Hanafi interpretation and closed the door to fresh interpretations.[5] The Sultans enacted from time to time certain *Iradés* and Firmans, or Royal Commands, and issued certain regulations and laws known as *Qanuns.*[6] These *Qanuns* could in no way be opposed to the principles of the Sacred Law but had to be in harmony with it. They were often based on three secondary sources of Muslim jurisprudence: the *Ijmâ'* or 'Consensus' of the Muslim community, the *Qiyâs* or "the analogical deductions of jurists", and the *Ijtihâd.*[7] These *Qanuns* belonged to the second category of laws ruling the subjects of the Ottoman Empire.

A third category of laws was embodied in the *Capitulations* (Droit Capitulaire) which regulated the relations of non-Muslim and foreign communities in the Ottoman Empire and were of an international character.[8] Except in very special cases, the non-Muslim communities in the Ottoman Empire were not subject to the *Shari'a* law. When Muhammad II conquered Constantinople, he found that the Christians and other non-Muslim Communities had their own legal systems and tribunals in which justice was administered by the spiritual heads of those Communities or their representatives. Their laws were based partly on Greco-Roman laws and partly on the Byzantine Civil Law of Justinian. He also found "a large number of foreign colonies, each with a well-defined legal status, which had been conceded to them by the Byzantine Emperors, and with distinct courts and court machinery and laws, and enjoying privileges and immunities."[9]

Immediately after the conquest of the city, *The Conqueror*, by confirming the practices of his predecessors, established the principle of religious autonomy for his non-Muslim subjects in the administration of their own affairs.[10] He also granted commercial privileges to large foreign trading communities established in the Ottoman Empire. The economic interests of the Empire necessitated the presence of these communities.[11] The immunities or "privileges" came to be known as Capitulations.[12] The Egerton Manuscript No. 2817 in the British Museum shows the grant of "special privileges for residence and trade" to the Genoese inhabitants of Galata (the suburb of Constantinople) after the fall of that city on May 29, 1453. This Grant is dated June 1 of that same year.[13] Other Capitulations followed, the most famous among them being the one granted to Francis I of France, the first European King thus favoured by Sultan Sulaiman the Magnificent in 1535, according to which the French obtained considerable trading privileges in the Ottoman Empire.[14]

As far as the machinery of Justice was concerned in the Ottoman Empire, the Capitulations necessitated the establishment of special Consular courts having complete jurisdiction over the nationals of the country concerned. Non-Muslim nationals of foreign countries living in Turkey enjoyed extra-territorial privileges and were not subject to Ottoman law no matter how serious the gravity of the criminal act which they might commit.[15] In these Consular Courts, the Consul himself generally acted as Judge of First Instance with two assessors. The sentences passed were executed on Turkish territory. Hence the plea of the British Consul in Cyprus in 1844 that Her Majesty's Government may allow him to build a small prison near his Consulate.[16]

For nearly four hundred years, the *Qanuns* were the only secular legislation which existed side by side with the Muslim *Shari'a* Law. In the nineteenth century, because of the increasing impact of Western thought upon the Ottoman Empire and of the political pressure of the European Powers, and as a result of various attempts to reform Ottoman institutions, particularly the *Tanzimat,* a system of secular jurisdiction was introduced throughout the Empire. Only the Personal Status law remained under the *Shari'a* Law. At the beginning of the century, in order to make it possible for native merchants to compete successfully with foreign merchants who enjoyed the privileges and the protection conferred upon them by the Capitulations, the Ottoman Government created a Corporation of merchants under Charter *("Beratli")* which had the same privileges accorded to the foreign merchants.[17] In 1840, a new Penal Code was adopted based on the French penal code. In the same year, a special Tribunal called *Majlis-i-Ahkâm-i-'Adliyah* was instituted to deal with the cases of high state functionaries. A Commercial Code was promulgated in 1850, and in 1861 special Tribunals of Commerce were established to administer that code. One more civil law to be added to the foregoing list was the Ottoman law of nationality, issued on January 19, 1869, and specifying the conditions under which Ottoman Nationality could be lost or gained. According to the first article of this law, every individual born of an Ottoman father and mother or of an Ottoman father only, was an Ottoman subject ("sujet Ottoman").[18]

In 1869, the Ottoman civil laws were collected and codified into a Register called *"Majallat-al-Ahkam al-'Adliyah"* by a special committee of 'Ulemas and non-'Ulemas appointed for that purpose and called the *"Majallah Jami'iyati"*.[19] This Ottoman Civil Code contains a total of 1851 articles. Finally, in 1879, there was a whole reorganisation of the judicial system by the creation of a Ministry of Justice and of "regulated tribunals" or *Mehâkim-i-Nizâmiyeh.*[20] This judicial reorganisation was based on French jurisprudence and was an important step in the direction of the modernization of the Ottoman Empire.

The Porte started, also, a reorganisation of its administration units in the Arab provinces, after the massacres in Mount Lebanon and Damascus in 1860. Up until the first half of that century, the Arab *Eyalets* of Turkey had been Mosul, Baghdad, "Haleb" (Aleppo), Saida and "Sham" (Damascus) with a total estimated population of 500,000 in the chief towns.[21] In Arabia, there were the *vilayets* of Hijaz and the Yemen. Geographical Syria was divided into two *vilayets:* Aleppo[22] and "Sham". The *vilayet* of "Sham" did not include anymore the Lebanon. According to the new "Protocole" for Lebanon, submitted by the Ambassadors of Five Powers[23] to the Porte and accepted by the latter, Mount Lebanon was detached from Syria and became an autonomous *sanjak* ruled by a Mutasarrif.[24] The "Protocole" embodied the "Règlements Organiques" of June 9, 1861, replaced by that of the 6th September, 1864 and amended by the Protocol of July 28th, 1868.[25]

In 1887, because of the growing importance of Jerusalem, the Porte created the new administrative unit of the independent *Sanjak* of Jerusalem in the south of Palestine. This *sanjak* was detached from the *vilayet* of *"Sham"* and put under the direct control of the Porte. Meanwhile the town of Beirut was expanding, and its commercial prosperity increasing rapidly. Consequently, the Porte decided to establish, in 1888, the new *vilayet* of Beirut to which the four sanjaks of Latakia, Tripoli, Acre and Nablus were attached. Thus, from 1888 onwards, Syria was divided into three *vilayets* (Aleppo, "Sham" and Beirut) and two detached *sanjaks* (Lebanon and Jerusalem).

Although the "Nationality Law" was a significant change in the Turkish concept of nationality, nevertheless, the individual was not a citizen of the Empire but a subject of the Sultan, and, in certain cases, a " Consular protégé " of one of the Foreign Powers.[26] The subjects of the Sultan were either Muslims or non-Muslims. The non-Muslims, particularly the Christians, were considered as the *Dhimmis*, i.e. as the "tolerated" and "protected" people because they were *Ahl-al-Kitab* (i.e. the People of the Book). They were known, however, as the *ra'iyah*, i.e. as the "shepherded people".[27] The word *ra'iyah* in its original meaning is a respectable word. It is derived from the Arabic *ra'â,* "to shepherd" hence *râ'i,* a shepherd, i.e. "him who leads to pasture lands". Thus the *ra'iyahs* are "those (cattle or other animals) under the guidance of a *râ'i*".

In Ottoman parlance, however, the word *ra'iyah,* which applied at one time to all the subjects of the Sultan,[28] denoted, when applied to the Christians, an inferior and humiliating position compared with the Muslims. The Christians were tributary people whose life and property were under *"amân",* i.e. safe only by the good pleasure of their Turkish masters. The Christian was not to ride a horse or to carry arms, nor could he join the Ottoman army or be admitted into the civil service. He was outwardly distinguished by the colour of his dress, his headwear and his shoes. The dress itself was to be different from the clothes "worn by men of learning, piety and nobility".[29] There could be no equality between him and the Muslim. Although the inequalities were formally, i.e. "on paper", abolished by the Hatti-Humayun of 1856,[30] nevertheless, in practice, the old *"Millet* system" continued throughout the nineteenth century.

The word *Millet* is an Arabic word for which there is no equivalent in Western political terminology.[31] The *Millets* were actually the members of the non-Muslim religious communities living in the Ottoman Empire who had already been granted a wide scope of cultural and civil autonomy by Muhammad, the Conqueror. First in importance among these *Millets* was the *Millet-i-Rum* which comprised all the Greek-Orthodox Christian subjects of the Sultan. The next in importance were the Armenian *Millet,* the Jewish *Millet,* the Roman Catholic *Millet* and the Maronite *Millet.* The "nationality" of every *"ra'iyah"* in these *Millets* was the particular religious denomination to which his *Millet* belonged. "In Syria", wrote Chevrillon, "individuals of the same race under the influence of different religious ideas are separated in distinct groups which are rightly called *Nations* and which are as different one from the other as the peoples of Europe are."[32] Writing to Sir Henry Bulwer from Beirut on April 25th, 1861, Lord Dufferin said: "...All over the Turkish Empire religious communities (Millets) are considered as individual nationalities."[33] In the French *Correspondances Diplomatiques* concerning the Asiatic provinces of the Ottoman Empire, there are many references to "la nation maronite", "la nation Grecque catholique". The Maronite patriarch is called "le Chef de la nation Maronite".[34] Indeed, M. de Petiteville, the French Consul General in Beirut, wrote in one of his despatches: "...cette Syrie ou le mot religion est synonyme du mot nation, voire même du mot Patrie."[35] Thus the line of demarcation was not along racial but along religious lines. The political identity of the Sultan's subjects was Ottoman (Osmanli) and his "nationality" was the *religion* of the Community to which he belonged, i.e. his *Millet*. The idea of nationality in the West European nineteenth century sense was almost non-existent in the Ottoman Empire.[36]

NOTES
AND REFERENCES

1. Towns and villages were divided into quarters called *mahallah* at the head of which was a Mukhtar—usually for every 20-50 houses. The number of Mukhtars in every town and village depended upon the number of their inhabitants.

2. Gibb and Bowen, p. 201. The other important officials in the government of a province were the *defterdar* or 'book-keeper' and the *Ketkhuda* or steward (called vulgarly *Kahya* or *Kikhya),* appointed on annual tenure, who held in his hands the other branches of administration. The "Kadi and the other religious dignitaries", as judges, administered justice according to Muslim Shari'a law and had "the right of sending protests and memorials direct to Istanbul". *Ibid.*

3. For a detailed and documentary account of these laws and the administrative units of the Ottoman Empire, see Young, vol. II, pp. 29-69.

    In the sixteenth and the beginning of the seventeenth centuries, the number of *eyalets* in the whole of the Ottoman Empire stood at 35 or 36 ; in the third quarter of the seventeenth century at 39.—Gibb and Bowen, p. 142.

4. Arnold, Sir Thomas and Guillaume A. (edits) *The Legacy of Islam,* (London, 1931...1943) p. 286.

5. "In a famous phrase it was said, 'the Gate of Interpretation has been shut'. The final touches of the immutable edifice of the Law were given, as far as the Hanefi section of Ottoman society was concerned, in the fifteenth and sixteenth centuries, with the composition of two books, 'The Pearls' and 'The Confluence of the Seas', in which were collected and reduced to order of a sort the opinions of all the most celebrated Hanefi doctors of times gone by."—Gibb and Bowen, pp. 22-23.

6. "All Ottoman society was divided into clearly defined groups and it was by virtue of their membership of such groups that the relationship of individuals to the government was conditioned. In order, therefore, to define the obligations entailed by this relationship, as also the status, the duties, the emoluments, the dress, &c., of persons actually in the government service, regulations were issued by the Sultans under the name *Kanun.*"—*Ibid.,* p. 23. See also Lybyer, pp. 157-159.

7. In its broad and general sense, *Ijtihad* is the decision which the Muslim judge is forced to reach as his personal opinion or discretion if he finds no guidance in the Qur'an or in the Sunna of the Prophet.

8. For a detailed account of the laws of the Ottoman Empire, see Young, in 7 volumes.

9. Khairallah, Ibrahim A., *The Law of Inheritance in the Republics of Syria and Lebanon* (Beirut, 1941), p. 149.

10. In this connection, it is interesting to note the following policy of

Great Britain in India: "Muhammadan law was applied to Muslims in British India as a matter of policy. This policy was the result of the adoption of a tradition inherited from the Mughal rulers of India, who applied the Hindu and Muhammadan laws to their subjects conformably with their own views, to safeguard and guarantee to each of these communities the practice of its own religion."—Fyzee, Asaf A.A., *Outlines of Muhammadan Law*. (Oxford University Press, 1949) p. 42.

11. « Au moyen âge, le commerce avec l'Orient se développa grâce à la concession aux étrangers de certains quartiers des villes les plus importantes dans lesquels il leur était permis de s'administrer eux-mêmes. Ce système était appliqué déjà dans l'empire byzantin et dans les royaumes fondés par les Croisés... »—Cahuet, Alberic, *La Question d'Orient dans l'Histoire Contemporaine, 1821-1905,* (Paris, 1905) p. 5.

12. "The Sultan (Muhammad II) had to regulate the judicial status of the non-Moslem population which formed the majority of the subjects of his new Empire. This he effected by a series of conventions with the chiefs of the various religious communities. To the Christians he conceded freedom of worship, the application of their own laws, and the administration of justice among themselves. At Constantinople, he invested a Greek Patriarch as the Supreme Judge in all the civil and religious affairs of the Greeks. To the Armenians, he accorded similar privileges."—De Rausas, Pelissié, *Le Régime des Capitulations dans l'Empire Ottoman,* (Paris, 1910). Introduction p. 10, cited in Ibrahim A. Khairallah's *The Law of Inheritance in the Republics of Syria and the Lebanon,* n. 45, p. 150. "Mehmed the Conqueror himself went so far to meet the susceptibilities of his non-Muslim subjects that one of his first acts after his capture of Constantinople was to invite the clergy of the Orthodox Church to elect a new Oecumenical Patriarch; and, when they presented George Scholarius as their candidate, the Ottoman Master of the Orthodox Christian World took care to ratify the election in accordance with the procedure that had been customary under the East Roman Imperial regime."—Toynbee, vol. VI, p. 203, n. 4.

It must be remembered that the Capitulations did not confer upon the Christians any rights or privileges which they did not already enjoy before the fall of Constantinople. Muhammad the Conqueror simply confirmed those rights and privileges, especially because a non-Muslim could not be within the pale of Muslim jurisdiction—and, hence, obtain justice in an Ottoman Court "where his testimony or that of his co-religionist would be held invalid."

13. The Grant is in Greek but carries on top of it the monogram (Tughra) of Sultan Muhammad II—The Conqueror—and at the bottom the name or signature, in Arabic script, of *Raghanus* or *Zaghanus*.

14. "Francis I of France actually cooperated with Sulayman the Magnificent in naval operations against the Hapsburg Power in the Mediterranean in 1543. France had been rewarded for her friendship already in 1535 by receiving 'capitulations' (i.e. a charter of trading rights)

from the Ottoman Government in advance of any other Western Power apart from the Italian republics. These 'capitulations' were confirmed and improved in 1740 as a reward for diplomatic services which the French Government had rendered to the Ottoman Government during the negotiations of the Belgrade peace-treaty between Turkey and Austria in 1739."—Toynbee, vol. II, p. 181, n. 2.

15. "The whole judicial, and even administrative problem was infinitely complicated by the capitulations, under which the various Great Powers possessed Courts, post offices and special privileges of their own." —Seton-Watson, R.W., *The Rise of Nationality in the Balkans,* (London, 1917) p. 101.

16. Great Britain, F.O. 78/580—*Turkey,* Despatch No. 13, dated Cyprus August 6, 1844 and addressed to the Earl of Aberdeen by Niven Kerr, states: "My Lord, ... I have to state to your Lordship that the British Consulate here is, I believe, the only one that has not a Prison attached to it...I am induced respectfully to submit to your Lordship's consideration my earnest hope that I may be authorized to construct a small Prison in the vicinity of this Consulate in which British subjects might be confined in conformity with the instructions lately sent me...A suitable prison might be erected here for a sum not exceeding 30..."

17. Young, vol. I, p. 224.

18. Young vol. II, pp. 223-229.

19. See Mahmasani, S., *Falsafat-al-Tashri' fi'l Islam,* (Beirut, 1946), pp. 70-75.

20. ... "The Nizamié Tribunals (were) composed of local and provincial Courts of First Instance and Appeal, with a Court of Cassation at Constantinople for the hearing of criminal and civil cases. At the same time, the Court of Appeal was divided into three Chambers, dealing with penal, civil, and commercial cases, respectively, and the Commercial Courts and Commercial Court of Appeal were transferred from the control of the Ministry of Commerce to that of the new Ministry of Justice." Great Britain, F.O. 371/345—Extracts from the Annual Report for Turkey for the year 1906—cited in Gooch, G.P. and Harold Temperley, *British Documents on the Origins of the War, 1898—1914,* Vol. V, p. 3.

21. *Ibid.,* p. 6. Farley, J. Lewis, *The Resources of Turkey,* p. 5. Farley gives the following statistics for population: "Mosul, 65,000, Baghdad 105,000, Aleppo 100,000, Beyrout 50,000 and Damascus 180,000."

22. The *vilayet* of Aleppo included four *sanjaks:* Marash, Urfa, Zor, and Aleppo.

23. Great Britain, Russia, France, Austria and Prussia.

24. "Its governor was necessarily a Christian and its administrative council consisted of four Maronites, three Druses, two Greek Orthodox

Christians, one Greek Catholic, one Moslem and one Metwali. The sanjak was divided into seven Kazas, of which four were Maronite, one Greek Orthodox, one Greek Catholic and one (Shuf) Moslem... The head of the police was always a Maronite. The Province enjoyed a system of taxation of its own." Great Britain, Admiralty—*A Handbook of Syria* (including Palestine), p. 243. See also Great Britain, Foreign Office, *Correspondence Relating to the Affairs of Syria*, 1860-61, Part II, p. 314.

25. For the full texts of the protocols and the "Règlements Organiques", see Young, vol. I, pp. 139-154.

26. For an account of the significance of the Ottoman Nationality Law, see Ghali, Paul, *Les Nationalités de l'Empire Ottoman à la suite de la guerre,* pp. 61-71.

27. It is to be noted that in the Old Testament, God is represented as a Shepherd and the people as his sheep or his flock and in the New Testament, Christ speaks of himself as the "good shepherd".

28. P. Rizzis was a Maltese who wanted to change his British nationality and become Austrian, while still living in Port Said (considered Ottoman territory) In taking up his case, the British Consul in Port Sa'id wrote to the Foreign Office: "In the Ottoman Dominion, every man is either a Consular protégé (Himaya) or a native subject (Ra'ya). If I inform the Egyptian Government that I have withdrawn protection (Himaya) from Mr. P. Rizzis, the latter at once becomes a Ra'ya until he can obtain other Consular protection."—Great Britain, F.O. 78/5238—*Turkey: Egypt*—Letter of D.A. Cameron, British Consul in Port Said, dated June 10, 1902 to the Marquess of Lansdowne. See also *Al-Manar,* vol. XVII, Part 7 (June 23, 1914), pp. 534-539.

29. "Christians must not mount on horseback in the towns: they are prohibited the use of yellow slippers, white shawls and every sort of green colour. Red for the feet and blue for the dress, are the colours assigned them. The Porte has just renewed its ordinances to reestablish the ancient from of their turbans; they must be of a coarse blue Muslim, with a single white border."—Volney, M.C.—F., *Travels in Syria and Egypt During the Years 1783, 1784 and 1785* (Perth, 1801) vol. II, p. 263. (Translation from the French).
    When Mr. John Barker was appointed British Consul in Aleppo in 1803, the Sultan issued a *Firman* recognizing him as Consul. Part of that *Firman* reads thus: "And if he shall wish to travel by land or by sea, no one shall...annoy him about *his riding on horseback, nor for his costume,*...And in places which may be unsafe, it shall be lawful for him *to wear a white turban, gird on a sword, have and carry bows and arrows...spurs to his boots*...without being hindered by an Kadee, Beylerbeg, or other person."—(the italics are the author's.)—Barker, Edward B.B., *Syria and Egypt under the Last Five Sultans of Turkey,* vol. II, pp. 322-323.

30. The word *ra'iyah* was abandonned and replaced by the word *Tab'ah* (from the Arabic *"tabi'a",* meaning literally to follow).

31. The Arabic word *Millah* means *Shari'ah* or religion. The Qur'an speaks several times of the *Millah* of *Ibrahim*, i.e. the religion of Abraham. (See Sura 2: The Cow and Sura 3: The Family of Imran). Later, the word was used to denote the people of the same religion.

32. Chevrillon, André, *Conférence Sur la Syrie*, (Rouen, 1897) p. 18.

33. Great Britain, Foreign Office, *Correspondence Relating to the Affairs of Syria*, 1860-61, Part II, p. 191.

34. The Patriarchs of the various Christian denomination were called by the Turks *Millet Bashi*, i.e. literally, the head of the nation.

35. Paris, *Archives du Ministère des Affaires Etrangères, Turquie—Beyrouth—1888*, Despatch No. 13 of March 25, 1888: "Notes Sur la Syrie". Among other particulars which an Osmanli had to fill in his *Tezkéré* or Passport, was the nature of his *Millet*.

36. "The Ottoman Empire began as the very opposite of a national State. It is not called after any people who inhabit it, but after the prince who founded it—Osman. It is true that Osman and his tribe were Turks; but they were only one out of a dozen Turkish States in Anatolia, and their Turkish neighbours were their most formidable rivals and enemies...

   "The cultivation of national consciousness by the Ottoman Turks was partly an imitation of older nationalist movements in Europe and partly the spontaneous product of similar conditions..." Great Britain, *Handbooks Prepared under the Direction of the Historical Section of the Foreign Office*, No. 96 c & d., *The Rise of the Turks—the Pan-Turanian Movement*, pp. 16-17.

CHAPTER III

ANTI-TURKISH SENTIMENT IN ARAB LANDS

Part 1 — Causes and Antecedents

The second half of the nineteenth century was the most decisive phase in the history of the Ottoman Empire ever since May 29, 1453 when the victorious troops of Muhammad II, 'The Conqueror' stormed their way into Constantinople. The once great Empire of the Ottomans which stretched from the gates of Vienna to the shores of the Caspian Sea and from the Persian Gulf to Aden and through the Red sea and north Africa to almost the Atlantic ocean, entered its last stages of decay and ruin.[1] All the evils of its autocratic regime were unveiled. Only through a proper knowledge of this background is it possible to understand the full significance of the awakened consciousness of the Arabs as to their fate and future destiny. The Empire was moving speedily towards final disintegration unless immediate steps were taken to infuse a new life into its internal organization and administration. From the first quarter of the nineteenth century onwards, a group of enlightened Turks were becoming increasingly aware of the necessity of rejuvenating the old and out-moded institutions and administrative machinery of their Empire. They were called the "New Ottomans". The period during which these "New Ottomans" struggled to achieve reforms in their country is known as the period of the *Tanzimat* or the *Tanzimat-i-Khayriyah* ("Beneficent Legislation") an expression which was apparently first used in the days of Mahmud II, (1808-1839). The basic reform projects, however, were not carried out.[2]

The truth is that none of the Sultans who issued the Hatti-Humayuns ever seriously considered becoming constitutional monarchs, nor did they want any intervention by the European Powers in their internal affairs. Indeed, how could any Sultan agree to any check on his sovereignty, whose official titles included such prerogatives and honorifics as "the Prince of the Faithful", "the Shadow of God on Earth", "the Vicegerent of the Prophet", "the Ruler of the Two Seas", "the Monarch of the Two Lands", and "One by whose birth creation had been honoured and the moon of happiness had risen"?.[3]

Harold Temperley wrote: "The heath of the Turkish Empire depended on three factors: on the ability of the Turks to reform; on the willingness of the Christian subjects to acquiesce in the process; and on the readiness of the Great Powers to help or hinder this evolution. No one of these factors sufficed by itself... But the Great Powers could not save Turkey. She alone could save herself, and reconcile her Christian subjects to her by reform. As will be seen, the Turks in fact waxed weaker and weaker, and the Christians stronger and stronger.."[4]

Anti-Turkish sentiment in Arab lands in the nineteenth century was a product of divers causes. The immediate causes were due to the rapid increase in the deterioration of the Turkish Government and to Western influences of various kinds. Under the impact of Western education, the infiltration of Western political ideas, the intercourse of commerce, the introduction of the material goods and the comforts of life, and through travel abroad and personal contacts with the West, the inhabitants of the Near East were slowly waking up to a new world of progress and power which was taking shape in the West, in sharp contrast to the state of stagnation and ignorance in which the Ottoman Empire was submerged.

But in the nineteenth century, there was as yet no "Arab Question" in international politics. Indeed, the word "Arab" itself as a designation for the inhabitants of the Arab provinces of the Ottoman Empire rarely occurs in the books and documents of the period. The general terms "Muhammedan" and "Christian" were used to describe the majority and minority inhabitants of this area. For Syria, the geographic appellation "Syrian" was sufficient. The word "Arab" was mainly reserved for the Bedouins of the desert and for all the non-town dwellers in the Near East. As to the great majority of the Muslim subjects of the Sultan, whether

Turks or Arabs, they were "brothers in the Faith", i.e. they were Muslims before being Turks and Arabs.[5]

Moreover, "the various races of which the subject populations were composed were not to be welded into a nation; and this, for the reason that the ruling class...on the one hand represented the political domination of Islam, and on the other was isolated by its constitution from all the ruled of whatever faith."[6] At the same time, the ruled and subject populations were in turn organized into semi-independent bodies, and as Gibb and Bowen have pointed out, "any wider allegiance that the individual members of these units might entertain was religious rather than political".[7]

However, the desire for local independent Government did appear in different parts of the Ottoman Empire, principally in Arabia, in Egypt and in Lebanon, but for very different reasons. The steps taken and the methods used were according to the exigencies of the time and the circumstances of the day.

In Arabia, the temporary successful attempt which was made to throw off the Turkish domination was the work of the Wahhabis. The anti-Turkish agitation was an entirely Muslim movement, and for certain reasons entirely anti-Western. The wrath of the Wahhabis was directed against what they considered to be the religious laxity and corruption of the Ottoman Government and the Ottoman Sultan himself, "including its ungodly inclination towards the filthy devices of the Frankish infidels," i.e. towards introducing reforms on Western lines.[8] The study of the origins of anti-Turkish sentiment in Arabia has hitherto been one of the neglected chapters of modern Arab history. It is often forgotten that a great blow to the already tottering foundations of the Ottoman Empire was delivered by Emir Muhammad Al-Sa'ud when he triumphantly entered Mecca in 1806 and had the public prayers read in his name instead of in the name of Sultan Selim III. Jean Raymond who was at the time the French Consul in Baghdad reported: "L'esprit de conquête s'est répandu dans tous les rangs, et le souvenir de l'ancienne puissance des Arabes semble avoir fait revivre jusque dans le cœur le plus faible le doux espoir de se voir encore gouverner par les princes de sa nation. Le passage suivant vient à l'appui de ce que j'énonce : l'autre jour un Wahaby disait d'un ton prophétique, 'le temps s'approche ou nous verrons un Arabe assis sur le trône des Califes; nous avons assez longtemps langui sous le joug d'un usurpateur' ".[9]

Although temporarily defeated between 1810 and 1817 by Muhammad 'Ali Pasha, the Wahhabis continued to grow in strength, though less aggressive than before, and completely regained their power at the beginning of the twentieth century, once more capturing Mecca in 1924, this time from King Husain.

The next move to separate the Arab world from Turkish sovereignty came from Muhammad 'Ali Pasha between 1830 and 1841 when his forces occupied Syria and advanced as far as Kutahiya in Asia Minor. There is no historical evidence however, to support the nationalistic aspect of the struggle, that of Arabs versus Turks. Muhammad 'Ali Pasha's goal was not the establishment of an *Arab* Empire in opposition to an Ottoman Empire, much as he may have professed, for ulterior motives of his own, pro-Arab sympathies and pro-Arab support. "An Arab racial movement in Egypt and Syria a hundred years ago would have been contrary to the whole trend of Oriental thought in those days. The world in which Muhammad Ali found himself was medieval in the widest and most inclusive sense of the word. All true believers were members of one big fraternity and they were all equal."[10]

Muhammad 'Ali Pasha's dominating and ambitious Albanian personality aimed at making Egypt independent of the Sultan and possibly at the actual conquest of the Ottoman Empire. While for nearly ten years he occupied and ruled the *vilayet* of Syria, he failed in his ultimate purpose and was finally compelled by British naval and military intervention to withdraw into Egypt. However, by the Firman of June 1, 1841, and the second Treaty of London of July 13, 1841, Muhammad 'Ali Pasha was confirmed as the hereditary Pasha of Egypt.

It is true that the Pasha was to be under the suzerainty of the Sultan, but in actual practice, Egyptian administration politically, economically and even militarily became almost completely autonomous. The Pasha was master of his own house.

In Maronite Lebanon, anti-Turkish sentiment was fostered by several factors such as Western education, the political ideals of the French Revolution, revival of Arabic language and literature, the printing press, the publication of Arabic newspapers, travel abroad and the return of Lebanese emigrants from the United States. But anti-Turkish agitation in this province of the Ottoman Empire was not due merely to those factors; it was primarily due to the fact that the Christians considered themselves like an alien island in the ocean of Turkish Muslim sovereignty. They simply did not feel "at home" under Turkish Government. It was not *their* Government. Towards the middle of the nineteenth century, the Maronites of Lebanon were provided with an additional reason to fear the Turks and to hope and work for their liberation from their Turkish masters: the massacres of 1860. Naturally, after the tragic events of that year, the Maronites never ceased to work for their complete separation from the Ottoman Empire and the establishment of Lebanon's independence. At the same time some foreign protection was necessary and it was obvious that in the case of Lebanon, that protection had to come from France, the traditional protector of the Maronites in the Near East. But the conclusion reached, that the upheaval of 1860 was "the decisive event of the nineteenth century" and that as a result of it "the seed of patriotism was sown, and a movement came into being whose inspiration was Arab and whose ideal was national instead of sectarian",[11] is misleading and entirely unwarranted. The anti-Turkish sentiment which grew in Lebanon was mainly a Maronite-Lebanese affair and cannot be considered in anyway as a national rising of all the Arabs in the Arab Near East against their Turkish masters. The vast majority of Muslims in the Asiatic and European territories ruled by the Sultan did not desire at that time to overthrow his rule.

It must also be remembered that the Christians of Lebanon had more frequent and more numerous contacts with the West than the rest of the Arab Near East had; hence Lebanon acted as a gateway for the entry of Western influences into the Asiatic provinces of the Ottoman Empire. It was natural that the process of Westernization should have been fostered by the Christians of the Ottoman Empire whether they were the Greek Orthodox Christians of the Balkan peninsula or the Maronites and Latin Christians of the Arab provinces. As Christians, they looked upon the Christians of the West and particularly upon the French as the leading lights in the progress of Western civilization.

Another important reason why the Christians of Lebanon were the principal channel through which the impact of the West on the Arab Near East was felt more strongly than, perhaps, through any other channel, was commercial intercourse with the West. This was particularly true in Lebanon and Syria and more in Lebanon than in Syria because of its geographic location and its past history when in the days of the Phoenicians the country was the foremost trading centre between the East and the West. It must also be remembered that under the Turks, "before 1856 Jews and Christians could not legally acquire land in Syria and until 1867 a similar prohibition applied to the case of all foreigners"[12] As a result, many Christians lived in towns and engaged in trade. Others came and joined them now. In the long run, most of the prosperous merchants all over the Empire were the Christians. Consequently, as Professor Arnold Toynbee has so correctly pointed out, "as merchants on the grand scale, they entered into commercial relations with the Western World and acquired a first-hand knowledge of Western manners and customs and Western languages".[13] There is no doubt that the growth of commercial prosperity accelerated the process of Westernization in Arab lands. Speaking of Beirut, in the middle of the nineteenth century Gregory Wortabet[14] wrote. "Its shops and stores are well provided from the factories of Europe and America. The produce of the Indies he (the traveller) finds in almost every street. Suspended on a rope from the verandahs of the various shops, he will see exposed for sale New England drills, Manchester greys, Scotch zebras, French silks, Swiss handkerchiefs, etc., and all bearing the stamps of the various factories where they are manufactured...Those who knew Bayroot twenty years back and the condition of its inhabitants, will acknowledge the midnight and midday difference between 1835 and 1855.[15]

"A few years ago" wrote Lewis Farley, "our principal merchants were foreigners, now they are natives; they now do all the exporting and importing business, and to them foreign ships come consigned. A few years ago, they lived in small houses, dingy and gloomy...but now they have built new houses, spacious and splendid, with garden lots, and furnished them in Europeo-

Oriental style... A few years back, men and women, beyond the circle of near connexions never associated, but now a more European life is being introduced in that respect...A few years ago, all the shipping of the place was the lateen sailed boats, which went up and down the coast with fish or fruits, or some other produce of the country...But now look at the roadstead of Bayroot and see its tonnage; gaze on the almost daily steamers that touch there from all parts of Mediterranean..."[16]

One more illustration of the type of change and Westernization which was taking place in Lebanon is worth recording here. It is taken from the "Report for 1893-4", entitled *Lebanon Schools,* written by the Reverend Dr. Carslaw of the Foreign Mission of the Church of Scotland. Dr. Carslaw in his capacity as a medical missionary had been transferred to the village of Shuwair in Lebanon. The above-mentioned report was written soon after his return — on April 30, 1894 — from a lecture tour in Scotland. Dr. Carslaw writes: "On our way up the mountain, we noticed a great improvement in the villages we passed through. Building operations were going on in many of them. Houses were having the old clay roofs taken off, and new roofs of Marseilles tiles put on. The outside shutters of windows, too, were getting a coat of green paint, and everything spoke of comfort and prosperity. In Shweir itself, too, we found things in the course of being changed; new houses are being built—those that are finished are roofed with tiles. Eighteen years ago there was not a tiled roof in the whole district, and at Shweir at that time there were only two houses that had glass windows; now glass windows are common, being looked upon as a necessity. Shweir has now a municipality, which has been working wonders. Streets have been paved, the fountains have been opened up, and their channels altered where necessary in order to avoid impurities, and iron pipes have been put in all of them. Quite recently, too, the municipality have fixed up four kerosine lamps to light up the principal street, and we saw them lighted one night. Workmen and labourers will no longer work for the same wages as they did a few years ago, and as wages rise, everything else seems to rise too.

"This appearance of prosperity seems to be caused by the return of a great number of Syrians who, a few years ago, emigrated to Brazil, the United States, and Australia. Having in various ways obtained large sums of money, they have returned with the intention of enjoying life so long as the money lasts. Of course, the old houses that their fathers lived in are not good enough for their descendants, who have been over half the world, and have seen so much. So the old houses must come down, new ones must be built, chairs and tables and all modern conveniences must be introduced, so that old manners and customs are being rapidly changed."

The new articles which the West introduced were most welcome for their utility as much as for their charm and novelty; they made the life of the Oriental more pleasant and more comfortable, altered his taste and raised his standard of living. But it must not be assumed that the commercial impact of the West made any deep impression on the vast majority of the Arab Muslims of the Near East. Its effects did not penetrate into the inner recesses of their hearts where their beliefs and their Faith lay treasured. The profounder issues remained untouched and unchallenged, no matter how glittering the outward changes appeared.

An important question remains to be asked: What rôle did Western education play in fostering anti-Turkish sentiment in the Muslim lands of the Near East? Almost every writer who has given an account of the "Arab Awakening" has emphasized the rôle of education in the "Awakening". These writers believe that the spread of Western political and democratic ideas in the Asiatic provinces of the Ottoman Empire was the work of foreign schools. It is true, of course, that French, American and Russian mission schools and other foreign missions such as the British Syrian Mission and the Prussian Mission of the Deaconess of Kaiserswerth, were actively engaged in educating the youth of the Near East. After 1831, the Jesuits opened schools in Beirut, Ghazir, Zahleh, Damascus and Aleppo; the Lazarist Fathers reopened their College in 'Aintura, and the American Presbyterians who first came in 1820, had, it appears, established by 1860 no less than thirty-three schools. But the two biggest educational institutions were the Syrian Protestant College founded in Beirut in 1866 and the Jesuit L'Université St. Joseph, established also in Beirut in 1875.

It is however, the contention of the present writer that while education has been a potent factor[17] in the awakening of the Arab Near East, the rôle of missionary education in the *national-political* enlightenment of the Arab youth in the second half of the nineteenth century has been greatly exaggerated. It must be remembered that many of the missionaries came to the Near East with the intention of spreading the Christian faith among the Muslims and, indeed, with the desire of converting some Christian denominations to their own brand of Christianity. Their schools were first and foremost *Christian* schools. The following words of Dr. Gregory Wortabet, one of the distinguished missionaries of the day represent the true spirit of most of the missionaries and the true purpose of their educational institutions. "I have now spoken of two powerful mediums, viz., preaching the gospel and medical influence, as great agencies in spreading the knowledge of true Christianity. They are helpmates, and one is necessary to the other...These, however, generally speaking, operate on adults... But there is another powerful medium which is exclusively brought to bear on the young, and which, if rightly handled, might under the blessing of God, be the means of regenerating Syria. I refer to the education of youths of this land. I do not mean the schools established by the various sects, where nothing but a corrupted liturgy is taught; but I mean Christian schools, where the Bible, 'the inheritance of the whole world', is a standard book, and where the youthful mind can drink deep of its pure waters...Now, I argue, that if such schools were established all over Syria, especially now that the cry for them is like a hurricane blowing over the land, who can estimate the results from them to the rising generation—a generation growing up in the 'admonition and nurture of the Lord'? Or who will doubt the happy results on Syria, socially and morally?".[18]

The religious activities of most of the foreign missions not only aroused the suspicions and fears of the vast majority of the Muslim inhabitants of these lands but they often fanned the flames of denominational and sectarian rivalries and even animosity,[19] so much so that the intervention of the foreign consuls became necessary at times to avoid political complications.[20] It is also unfortunately true that not all missionaries devoted their activities entirely to the religious field. With the exception of the American missions,[21] some missionaries of the Great Powers interested in the Near East considered it as part of their duty to enchance and foster the political prestige of their countries and for this purpose they were fully supported by their Governments.[22] The French educational institutions headed by the Jesuit mission took the lead by their zeal and enthusiasm in inculcating the love of France in the hearts of their pupils.[23]

But barring the patriotic interests of certain missionaries for their own countries, a glance at the curriculum of the mission schools will reveal that the subjects taught at that time had no bearing whatsoever on politics or nationalism. The main emphasis was on language, literature and mathematics, i.e. the three R's, and in addition, naturally, religious education. For example, the list of subjects taught at the Syrian Protestant College during its first year of existence, 1866-67, contained: Languages—Arabic, English, French, Turkish and Latin; Arithmetic, Algebra and Geometry, Ancient History of the Arabs, History of Religions and Bible study. There was a "Faculty" of thirteen teachers and a total of sixteen students, only three of whom were from Beirut.[24] Twelve years later, in 1878-79, the program of studies in the Collegiate Department offered the following courses: 1st year (Freshman)—Arabic Grammar, English Grammar and Literature, Algebra, Geometry, Holy Scriptures, Music, Composition, and Declamation; 4th year (Senior)—Astronomy, Mental Philosophy (sic!), Ethics, History, Geology, Botany or Zoology, Music, Composition, Declamation and the Holy Scriptures. (I have omitted the second and third years in order not to prolong unduly this discussion.) There were at this time 48 regular and 45 special students with only five students in the graduating class. The School of Medicine had 28 students with three in its fourth and last year, and there was one student studying Pharmacy.

The great contribution of most of these schools was to teach a small proportion of the rising generation to read and write. But, unfortunately, there wasn't much to read in Syria in those days[25] and during the latter part of the nineteenth century, the government imposed a rigid censorship on all foreign books and papers imported from abroad.[26] The truth is that most of the foreign schools and institutions were "selling their own goods" and vying with one another to gain the love of the largest number of students for their own national ends. The one exception was the Syrian Protestant College where there was no attempt at any "Americanization" whatsoever.[27]

However, we have to wait for the end of the nineteenth and the beginning of the twentieth centuries for the anti-Turkish sentiment to gather momentum and finally to break into open rebellion and war. But even at that time, the vast majority of the Muslim Arabs did not take part in any attempt to separate the Arab world from Turkish sovereignty. Only a small, enlightened, ambitious and, in many cases, non-Muslim minority, wanted to substitute Arab for Ottoman sovereignty. While due consideration and credit should be given to that enlightened minority, it must be emphasized that their opinion was in no way representative of the opinion of the vast majority of the Muslim Arabs who thought of Turkey primarily as Muslim and of the West primarily in terms of the material products of science and technology, but who were neither familiar nor sympathetic with the spirit and philosophy underlying the Western way of life.

NOTES
AND REFERENCES

1. "Sous Mahmoud et aux débuts du règne d'Abdul-Medjid, la Turquie était à peu près, selon l'image connue, comme un navire dont it faut renouveler la carène, la mâture, les voiles et l'équipage". Engelhardt, Ed., *La Turquie et le Tanzimat*, pp. 4-5.

2. It must not be supposed that between 1839 and 1876 no changes took place in the Ottoman Empire. Life in Europe was undergoing a great transformation. The slow moving tempo of the eighteenth century was being replaced by a fast moving pattern of progress based on industrialization and technology and new political doctrines inspired by the French Revolution. The jetsam and flotsam of western ideas, fads and fashions and new ways of living reached the Golden Horn, the western shores of Asia Minor and the Near East. Moreover, Ahmed Emin has recorded in his book *Turkey in the World War* (p. 26) that "in 1848, the era of revolution in Europe brought the Ottoman Empire a rich harvest of able men". "They came as fugitives", continues Dr. Emin, "Turkey refused to give them up, even though Austria and Russia threatened war. Many of them became Turks and entered the Turkish public service".—Thus, in many ways contacts increased with the Western world. But still at this time, introducing "Western civilization" in Turkey meant, on the whole, imitating and adopting the superficial and external trappings of that civilization. Panaretoff wrote in his *Near Eastern Affairs and Conditions*, (New Haven, 1922 p. 130): "European usages and customs found their way into the capital. The Sultan set the example of European dress, gave in his palace dinners, concerts and balls as any European ruler would have done". These and other superficial changes and veneers did take place here and there in Turkey and mainly in Constantinople. But they must not be confused with the reforms that men like Rashid Pasha and Midhat Pasha had in mind. They both wanted *constitutional reforms* of far reaching character by adopting the Western constitutional system of Government which in the words of Midhat Pasha, has been "one of the principal causes of the progress of nations", for "Turkey", he added, "ranks among the Great Powers and in order to obtain this object and to march on a footing of equality with its neighbours in the progress of sciences, she must need follow the same method."—Midhat, 'Ali Haydar, *The Life of Midhat Pasha*, p. 80.

    See also Karal, Enver Ziya, *Osmanli Tarihi*, VI cilt: *Islahat Fermani Devri, 1856-1861* (Ankara, 1954); Contenson, Baron Ludovic de, *Les Réformes en Turquie d'Asie, La Question Arménienne, La Question Syrienne ;* and Bailey, Frank Edgar, *British Policy and the Turkish Reform Movement, 1826-1853*.

3. Sarkis, Salim, *Sirr Mamlakah*, p. 5. "The Ottoman Government, when it undertook to place the Empire on a new foundation, was neither entirely sincere in its professions, nor did it clearly understand what it was about. It accepted the announcement of great, immense, and

sudden reforms, less with a desire to reinvigorate Turkey than to gain Europe. It was less occupied with the laws it was to make than with the newspaper articles it would produce. It consequently undertook too much, too suddenly, and got confused amidst the novelties it promulgated. An uncertainty between the old and the new everywhere prevailed, and still prevails. A Pasha said to me the other day, 'What am I to do? I govern a province, and the grand Vizier sends me an order which is framed on the new ideas that we profess. The Sheikh-ul-Islam complains against me because I do not act upon the old laws, which with him are still sacred. I say the two things are incompatible; and I am told I must follow our own usages, but I must give them a new dress. I don't know what I am about.' "—Sir Henry Bulwer, British Ambassador in Constantinople, in a Report on the Finances of the Turkish Empire, August, 1861—cited by Madden, Richard Robert, in *The Turkish Empire*, pp. 407-408.

In September 1830, M. Michaud wrote from Pera (Istanbul) on the subject of *La Réforme en Turquie:* "... Pour arriver d'ailleurs à une civilisation quelconque, il faudrait en avoir au moins une première idée et savoir ce que c'est; ici notre civilisation est tout à fait comme une terre inconnue, comme un monde nouveau; il est difficile de marcher droit vers un but qu'on ne connaît pas, et de marcher vite lorsqu'on ne connaît pas précisément où l'on va. Il n'y a point de véritable zêle parce qu'il n'y a point de conviction; le sultan, lui-même, ne croit pas toujours à sa propre révolution; de là ces hesitations qui ressemblent au découragement et qui font encore quelquefois que tous les projets de réforme sont abandonnés."—Poujalet, M., *La France et la Russie à Constantinople,* (Paris, 1853) pp. 148-149.

4. Temperley, *England and the Near East, The Crimea,* (London, 1936), "Foreward", p. VII.

5. Rashid Rida, founder of the Arabic periodical *Al-Manar* wrote in an article entitled "Races in the Ottoman Empire" that Arab unity is based on Islam and on the Arabic language and that the Arabs have been the last among all peoples to develop race consciousness and race prejudice, for the vast majority among them are Muslims and as Muslims they are conscious only of their "religious nationality". *Al-Manar,* vol. 17, No. 7, July 1914, p. 534.

"Islam is the fatherland of the Muslim" *("Al-Islam watan al-Muslim").* See 'Azzam, 'Abdu'l Rahman, *Al-Risalah al-Khalidah* (Cairo, 1946) p. 105. 'Azzam adds, on p. 141: "The Muslim's fatherland *("watan")* has no geographic boundaries, it expands with the spreading of his faith".

6. Gibb and Bowen, vol. I, p. 159.

7. *Ibid.,* p. 159.

"Islam is a faith that has never encouraged the growth of nationality. Its universal character has toned down, rather than accentuated, racial and cultural differences that might have hardened into national qualities...The only common factors in the Arab World (in Turkish days) were unity of language and unity of subjection. The Syrian and the Egyptian, the nomad and the fellah, the learned and the populace, were too much divided by customs, by ideas, by tradition, to be at all willing to recognize anything common but religion..."—Dodwell, H., *The Founder of Modern Egypt*, pp. 127-128.

8. Toynbee, A.J. and Kirkwood, K.P., *Turkey*, (New York, 1927), p. 42.

9. Raymond, Jean, *Mémoire sur l'origine des Wahabys, sur la naissances et sur l'influence dont ils jouissent comme nation (1806)*. (La Société Royale de Géographie d'Egypte, 1925), p. 34.

10. Rustum, Asad, J., *The Royal Archives of Egypt and the Origins of the Egyptian Expedition, 1831-1841*, p. 85. Dr. Rustum adds, however, that "through his contact with Europe and European officers, Ibrahim Pasha seems to have been personally convinced of the soundness of the nationalistic philosophy...In this sense Ibrahim Pasha certainly deserves the place of honour in the history of nationalism in the Arab East." *Ibid.*, p. 96.

It seems that in France, a number of deputies believed in the policy of supporting Muhammad 'Ali Pasha and helping him to break the Ottoman Empire into two halves, one Turk and one Arab and thus forming a *"Royaume Arabe"*. But Freycinet adds that while such a policy was a sign of the times, it was that of a "romantic school" and the conception itself was "un peu chimérique"—Freycinet, C. de, *La Question d'Egypte*, p. 76.

"It is certain that Mehemet Ali never meant to be a pan-Arab, but... he meant to increase his power."—See Temperley, *The Crimea*, pp. 96 and 419-422.

11. Antonius, George, *The Arab Awakening*, p. 60.
Indeed, the Turks themselves have been accused of conniving at those disorders and bloodshed. "After the withdrawal of Ibrahim Pasha and the restoration of Ottoman rule, the Sultan's Government set itself deliberately to foment religious conflict in order to make the traditional autonomy of Lebanon unworkable and so to create an excuse for the establishment of direct Ottoman rule over the Mountain."—Hourani, A. H., *Syria and Lebanon*, p. 31.

12. Great Britain, *A Handbook of Syria.*.p. 250.

13. Toynbee, Vol. II, p. 224.

14. Wortabet, Gregory, *Syria and the Syrians*, Vol. I, pp. 35-43.

15. Seven years later, Lewis Farley wrote: "For some years past, a very extraordinary improvement in the commercial prosperity of Syria has been everywhere apparent...At Alexandretta, Latakia, Tripoli, Sidon, Kaiffa and Jaffa, signs of an increasing commerce have been also evident..." Farley, Lewis, *The Resources of Turkey*, pp. 206-207.

16. "No longer than fifteen years ago, there was scarcely any steam communication between Beyrout and Europe, now...English steamers run regularly between Beyrout and Liverpool...The line of steamers belonging to the 'Messageries Impériales' and Austrian Lloyd's Company has also been increasing."—Farley, pp. 209-210.

17. As early as 1843, the French Ambassador in Constantinople, M. Bourquency, writing to M. Guizot about the Jesuit educational activities said: "Le rôle des forces intellectuelles en Orient prend chaque jour une importance plus vraie, plus grande ; et nous ne pouvons apporter trop de vigilance et de soin à organiser dès l'origine à régulariser l'emploi et les tendances de ces forces — nous dont l'influence et l'honneur, dans ces contrées, semblent, aussi bien par la puissance des traditions que par la force même des choses intimement liés à leurs dévelopement et à leur progrès."—France, *Archives du Ministère des Affaires Etrangères, Turquie, 1843-44.* Despatch No. 130/60, vol. 290, pp. 67-68.

18. Wortabet, pp. 205-206.

19. *Ibid.,* pp. 47-49. The Muslims rarely sent their children to Mission or foreign schools. They kept aloof from Christian institutions of learning. They wanted an education which was Arab and Muslim in form and in spirit. One of the Muslim schools which was founded in Beirut in 1895 by Shaikh Ahmad 'Abbas al-Azhari was known as *Al-Kulliyah al-'Uthmanîyah al-Islamîyah.* Many of the Arab Muslim political leaders and secret society organizers were graduates of that school.

20. The following document which the author found in the Public Record Office in London is most illuminating and worth quoting in full:
"Sir,

I have received your despatch No. 36. of the 10th ultimo together with its several inclosures.

With reference to one of those inclosures, namely your despatch No. 37 to Sir Stratford Canning on the subject of the protection which in consequence of the appeal made to you on the part of the American Missionary, Mr. Smith, you had thought it right to afford to the Protestant converts from the Greek Faith in the Hasbeya and adjoining districts, I have to inform you that Her Majesty's Government perfectly approve of your affording general and efficient protection to all Christians in Turkey who may appeal to you against the oppression of the Mussulman Authorities of the Porte. But in admitting the propriety of acting upon this general principle, Her Majesty's Agents should observe the utmost discretion both with regard to carrying interference with the Mahomedan faith beyond due bounds, and to appearing to give official support to those efforts which American and other Missionaries are now making in the Ottoman territories to draw off the votaries of other Christian sects to Protestantism.

Abstractedly, Her Majesty's Government would naturally desire to see the tenets of the Anglican Church embraced by persons of all faiths, whether Mahomedan, Greek or other. But it would be highly injudicious and improper and not a little hazardous for the peace of the world, were Her Majesty's Government to govern their own actions, or to permit British official Agents to govern theirs, by this principle. Such a mode of proceeding could scarcely fail to excite the active hostility of all other religions and sects.

The attention of the Emperor of Russia, one of the most powerful heads of the Greek Church, has already been awakened to the conversions which Protestant missionaries in the East are actively endeavouring to effect, and have succeeded in effecting, from the Greek Church ; and it is unnecessary to observe to you that the religious hostility or active interference of Russia in the East is not to be desired.

You will therefore carefully abstain from any act which might be construed into giving support or countenance to the conversions from the Greek faith to Protestantism which foreign missionaries in Turkey are now labouring with injudicious zeal to effect ; but you will at the same time not relax your exertions whenever they can be properly employed in protecting Christians from Mahomedan persecution."—*F.O. 78/575, Turkey* (Diplomatic), January to December 1844, The Earl of Aberdeen to Consul Rose (Beirut), Despatch No. 10, dated September 19, 1844.

21. According to the testimony of the French representative himself:
     "J'ai longtemps cherché quel était le but poursuivi par les Americains en venant évangéliser ici. Je me suis convaincu à la longue que leur seul mobile était la propagande religieuse. Derrière-pensée politique je n'en vois réellement pas." France, *Archives du Ministère des Affaires Etrangères, Turquie—Beyrouth, 1888.* Le Vte de Petiteville— French Consul General in Beirut writing to the Ministry of Foreign Affairs, Paris. Despatch No. 13—Letter of March 25, 1888.

22. Rashid Rida in his editorial in *Al-Manar* of December 28, 1913 launched a violent attack against the evil influences of Western education in Muslim lands—an education which teaches the young Arabs to despise their ancestors and glorify everything foreign—in the name of civilization. These young men according to *Al-Manar* were the peaceful army used by the Westerners for the "peaceful penetration and conquest of Muslim lands".—*Al-Manar,* vol. 17, pp. 8-9.

23. Charmetant has quoted Gambetta's words to him: "Le Cardinal Lavigerie et ses missionaires (in Syria) ont rendu à la France plus de services qu'un corps d'armée", adding "Oui, plus de service qu'un corps d'armée, plus qu'une escadre de notre flotte."—And the Apostolic Delegate himself wrote: *"Il nous faut la Syrie toute entière, de Gaza à Adana, et du Liban à Mossoul"*—
     Mgr. Charmetant, protonotaire apostolique, directeur général de l'Oeuvre des Ecoles d'Orient, *Constantinople, Syrie et Palestine, Lettre Ouverte à Nos Hommes d'Etat,* pp. 13 and 35 respectively.
     On October 14, 1887, the French Minister of Foreign Affairs wrote to M. Petiteville, French Consul General in Beirut—in connection with the eighty-two scholarships that France had offered for students in Syria to study in the Jesuit schools there—: "Lorsque les bourses ont été instituées en Syrie, on s'est proposé deux buts principaux. Le premier a été de se créer des clients au sein des familles parmi

lesquelles étaient choisis les boursiers. Le second but à été de stimuler l'ardeur et des chefs d'institution et des enfants vers l'étude de la langue française. Ces deux résultats ont été atteints en partie. Car nous nous sommes attachés un certain nombre de familles influents dont les plus jeunes membres ont été élèves sinon dans l'amour de la France, au moins dans la connaissance de sa langue et de son histoire."—France, *Archives du Ministère des Affaires Etrangères, Turquie,* vol. 30, despatch No. 51.

"The British consuls of Syria believe that the imperial interests of England are bound up with the missionary interests of the several Bible Societies, whose agents are established in Syria. They imbibe the polemics of the missionaries, and they adapt their politics to them."—Madden, p. 370.

24. The English examination questions of the Senior Class in 1871 included fifteen lines of simple English to be translated into Arabic and the following questions: "What is a Zone and where is the torrid Zone? What is the difference between principal and principle? State the difference between compare and contrast." The Senior History questions (in Arabic) for the year 1873 included the following: "Who were the Hyksos and when did they occupy Egypt? What evidence can you give that Babylon was the first among the inhabited countries of the world: What is the origin of the Kingdom of Assyria and how long did that Kingdom last?" (See *Catalogues of the Syrian Protestant College,* at the Registrar's Office of the American University of Beirut, Beirut, Lebanon.)

The program of the Presbyterian High School in Damascus embraced the following subjects: reading, Arabic grammar, Scriptures, history, geography, arithmetic and the English language. "The school duties commenced by reading a portion of the Scriptures, and prayer; and closed in like manner. This, in fact, is the plan on which the Protestant schools are conducted. The principals are generally the missionaries, who are assisted in teaching the higher branches, by a graduate of the 'Abaih seminary."—Wortabet, pp. 209-210.

25. "An estimate of the general want of instruction may be formed from the fact that the demand for books is so small in Syria that I could not find a bookseller in Damascus or Aleppo...Some of the books printed by the Egyptian Government, at the Bulaq Press, are sent to Syria, and are sold there, but the demand is small; they, however, have made their way into some of the schools, and into a few private families."—*Report on Commercial Statistics of Syria,* by John Bowring (Parliamentary Papers, 1840) quoted by Antonius, p. 38, n. 2.

26. The following stories may be apocryphal but they do indicate the state of mind of some of the censors, and their ludicrous ignorance. It is said that one of the Turkish censors in Beirut refused, at first, to let a Physics textbook be received by the Syrian Protestant College because he had noticed several times the word "revolution" in one of the chapters of that book! Another censor objected to a Chemistry textbook destined for the same College to enter the country—except

after much explanation—because he thought that the formula for water, H_2O stood for: Hamid ('Abdu'l) II is zero! See also Ramsaur, E.E., *The Young Turks*. pp. 104-105.

27. The attitude of Reverend Daniel Bliss, founder of the Syrian Protestant College (now the American University of Beirut) was a rare exception. He was greatly respected and admired by the peoples of the Arab lands for the tolerance, understanding and deep sympathy which he had for them. On December 7, 1871, when the cornerstone of College Hall was laid by the Honourable William Earl Dodge, Senior, Dr. Bliss said: "This College is for all conditions and classes of men without regard to colour, nationality, race or religion. A man white, black or yellow, Christian, Jew, Mohammedan or heathen, may enter and enjoy all the advantages of this institution for three, four or eight years; and go out believing in one God, in many Gods, or in no God. But, it will be impossible for anyone to continue with us long without knowing what we believe to be the truth and our reasons for that belief."—*The Reminiscences of Daniel Bliss* (New York, 1920), p. 198

CHAPTER IV

ANTI-TURKISH SENTIMENT IN ARAB LANDS

Part 2 — The Reign of 'Abdu'l Hamid
1876 - 1909

'Abdu'l Hamid was born on September 22, 1842 in the Palace of Dolma-Baghcheh, on the European shore of the Bosphorus. "...On Thursday, August 31, 1876, Abdu'l Hamid left the house of Perestu Hanum, the lady who had adopted him, and, accompanied by the Minister of War and a hundred and fifty soldiers on horseback, at half past eight in the morning arrived at the Imperial Palace at Stamboul, where the Ministers and high dignitaries were already assembled. At ten o'clock the boom of a hundred guns announced the deposition of Sultan Murad and the appointment of his brother Abdu'l Hamid. The new Sultan was then hailed as Padishah and embarked at Seraglio Point, followed by a great number of caiques belonging to the Court, and was conducted to the palace of Dolma-Baghshe, which had been quitted a few hours earlier by Sultan Murad and his family. Abdu'l Hamid had obtained his wish and was now undisputed Sultan of Turkey."[1]

The reign of 'Abdu'l Hamid saw one of the most disastrous phases of the Eastern Question; the Ottoman Empire suffered a greater dismemberment than ever before. Fear of the disintegrating effects of the external pressure exerted by the Great Powers and fear of internal rebellions made the Hamidian regime more tyrannical. 'Abdu'l 'Hamid himself had an inordinate fear of assassination and an almost pathological suspicion of those who surrounded him. On one rare occasion—November 30, 1878— he gave vent to his feelings by telling M. de Torey, the French military attaché at the French Embassy in Constantinople: "En ce pays d'intrigues... comment lutter toujours et contre tous ?"[2]

Under 'Abdu'l Hamid, suspicion between Arabs and Turks increased. He had already been greatly disturbed by the anti-Turkish agitation in Lebanon and the appearance of "revolutionary leaflets" in Beirut in the days when Midhat Pasha was the *Vali* of Syria. He was well aware of the growing feeling of discontent in his Asiatic possessions. Terrified of revolutionary activities and realizing that the administration of his Arab provinces was greatly decentralized, he tightened up the controls from Constantinople and more and more laid an iron grip on the government of those provinces. Thanks to the new invention of the telegraph, his capital was now in close touch with the principal cities of his provinces, and thanks also to the introduction of railway lines troops could move more quickly and more easily to possible trouble areas.

His fear of an Arab majority weakening the ruling Turkish element was heightened by his suspicion that the Arabs were working towards the establishment of an Arab Caliphate.[3] But at first he made several attempts to win the Arabs,[4] either through expensive gifts, or through excessively generous hospitality accorded to Arab leaders visiting Constantinople, or by appointing Arabs to high administrative and military posts in the Government,[5] and finally by the ingenious device of pan-Islamism. The dream of reuniting the Muslim world and rebuilding the Muslim Empire, had been very close to the hearts of many Muslim leaders throughout the world. "The notion, however, that the religious headship of Islam might be politically utilized was adopted by Abdu'l Hamid II... The persons supposed to have impressed him with the idea are Si Muhammad Zafir, a Marabout of Tripoli who had foretold his accession, this Marabout's cousin, Sheikh Asad, and a certain Abu'l Huda Effendi. They persuaded him that his predecessors had been mistaken in cultivating the friendship of European Christian Governments, and that his true course was to attempt to reunite Islam against Christendom."[6] 'Abdu'l Hamid was led to believe that if he placed himself at the head of the Muslims as the champion of Islam and the protector of the Muslims living under Christian Governments, the Sunni Muslims, Arabs and non-Arabs, would rally round the Ottoman Caliphate and support it fully and unconditionally. It is believed that the railway line between Damascus and Medina—the Hejaz Railway—which was built with the monetary contributions of Muslims throughout the world, had for one of its principal motives the winning of the friendship and support of Muslims throughout the world. Soon after the inauguration of the railway at Medina (September 1908), a leader in the *Times,* discussing the motives of 'Abdu'l Hamid, said: "He saw from the outset that the making of the line would strengthen the position he claims for himself as the spiritual head of Islam; and he perceived, perhaps even more acutely that the railway will have a very great strategic value, when it is linked up with the Anatolian system. It lies very near the flank of Egypt, and it affords a rapid means for the transport of troops towards those provinces of Arabia which have never been properly subjugated by Turkey."[1]

'Abdu'l Hamid need not have had any worries about his Arab subjects as far as the Caliphate was concerned. In his days, it was inconceivable to the vast majority of the Muslim Arabs not to support the Caliphate, because the support of the Caliphate was the support of Islam. Moreover, the thoughtful among them looked upon European designs on the Ottoman Empire with great alarm lest the Powers should eventually partition Turkey, which would mean the end of the Caliphate and of Arab existence in a Muslim Empire.

But, if in the realm of politics the Arabs as Muslims acquiesced in the excesses of 'Abdu'l Hamid's regime, they were nevertheless alienated by his tyrannical measures. 'Abdu'l Hamid, no doubt, realized that it was not possible to conduct the policy of his multi-national and theocratic Empire in accordance with nationalist principles and constitutional methods of government. Forced at the beginning of his reign into accepting Midhat Pasha's constitution, 'Abdu'l Hamid acted for a while as a Constitutional Monarch. The first Turkish Parliament met on March 18, 1877 in the great Reception Hall of Dolma-Baghcheh and heard the Sultan's speech from the throne. But that Parliament acquired the name of the "Yes-Sir" Parliament because it replied continuously "Yes, Sir", "Yes, Sir" *(Evet Efendim, Evet Efendim)* to all the suggestions and opinions of the Chairman who had actually been appointed (not elected) by 'Abdu'l Hamid himself, as "Speaker" of the House.[8] On February 14, 1878, by the Sultan's command, the Ottoman Parliament was dissolved *sine die*. As for the deputies, the more enlightened, more courageous and more outspoken in the criticism were ordered to leave Constantinople. Among them were a number of prominent Arab representatives. This humiliation of the representatives of the nation evoked no emotions of protest either among the Turkish public or in the Turkish press. Not long afterwards, Midhat Pasha and other Turks were either exiled or imprisoned or even murdered by orders of 'Abdu'l Hamid.[9]

One of the consequences of 'Abdu'l Hamid's policy was that reforms and reform movements and all anti-Hamidian opposition were driven either underground or beyond the boundaries of the Empire, particularly to Paris, London, Geneva and Cairo.[10] Hence, also, the rise of secret societies with the object of working for the introduction of reforms in Arab countries and, in some extreme cases, for the entire liberation of the Arabs from Turkish or any other alien domination.[11]

We have already seen in the previous chapter that after Arabia, in the nineteenth century, it was in Lebanon that anti-Turkish agitation developed and gathered strength, and it is almost certain that after 1876 the first reaction to 'Abdu'l Hamid's despotism and Pan-Islamism came also from that province of his Empire.

Two assertions are, however, unsupported by any serious historical evidence, namely: (a) that a small group of 'enlightened élite', through their secret society in Beirut, spread the seeds of Arab nationalism, and (b) that "the first organized effort in the Arab national movement" can be traced back to the activities of that group.[12] Unfortunately, the whole story has been exaggerated as far as the concept of "nationalism" is concerned. Perhaps it is worth recording here, briefly, the account which the author himself heard from the lips of the last surviving member of that small group of young "conspirators": the late Dr. Faris Nimr Pasha.[13] To begin with, Faris Nimr Pasha emphasized that the idea of "nationality" did not exist in the minds of the masses

of the people in the Near East at that time. All the ties and rela-
tionships and loyalties were denominational, primarily Muslim or
Christian. The Muslim was principally either Sunni or Shi'i and
the Christian was primarily either Maronite, Greek Orthodox,
Catholic or Protestant. National unity was impossible under the
circumstances. A young "enlightened élite", most of whom were
Christians,[14] and some of whom had studied at the Syrian Protestant College in Beirut, wanted first and foremost to emancipate
Christian *Lebanon* from the Turkish yoke. They formed a "secret
revolutionary society" which used to meet during certain evenings
on the rocky seashore, near the Pigeon Rocks, south of Beirut,
to exchange views and discuss ways and means of achieving their
objective.[15] What was uppermost in the minds of these young men
was their being humiliated and made to feel "inferior" by the
Turk. One of the sayings of the time was: "the Turk is 'riding
over' the Muslim and the Muslim 'riding over' the Christian!"
The Arab Muslim speaking of the Ottoman Empire could say:
"It is also *my* Empire", for it was a Muslim Empire and the Muslim felt at home in it. But the Christian was conscious most of
the time that he was only one of the *ra'iyah*. The Turkish Government could not be *his* Government.

It soon became evident to these young men that for the success of their goal the cooperation and support of the Muslims
was necessary. It was imperative that a common and united front
be presented to the Turks. The leading members of the secret
society joined the Masonic Lodge of Beirut and hoped in this
way to enroll notable Muslims in the Lodge and make them later
join their society. A few Muslims did join the Lodge and did
learn about the society but, according to Nimr Pasha, soon Muslims and Christians disagreed. Their unity was broken up and
"a wonderful opportunity lost".[16] What is significant is the concluding remark of Dr. Nimr Pasha that they became convinced
that between the Christians and the Muslims no agreement and
understanding could be reached on the expulsion of the Turks
from Lebanon and therefore no united action was possible. Other
secret societies were formed, some years later.

As to the enlightened Arab Muslims, they took a defensive
attitude towards the current of Westernization and European in-

filtration, particularly when they started to suspect that this infiltration of Western goods, Western ideas and Western ways of
life, backed by the political interests of the Powers, would eventually lead to the occupation of the Arab Near East by one or
more than one of the Western Powers. It must be recalled, in this
connection that Western colonial expansion in Africa and Asia
was in full tide between 1844 and 1900. The Muslim's answer
was to try to strengthen the influence of Islam both as a means
of progress and as a defensive mechanism against the West. They
had no thought of either destroying Ottoman sovereignty or seced-
ing from the Ottoman Empire. All that they asked for were political and economic *reforms* so that they might progress and place
themselves on an equal footing with the Westerners. On the other
hand, the vast mass of the illiterate, the peasants and the poor
continued to live their lives undisturbed by the new forces of
enlightenment.

An important point to remember is that the Muslim leaders
at the time were warning the Arabs to prepare themselves against
the encroachments of the West rather than encouraging them to
overthrow the Turkish regime. Leading Muslims, as well as the
vast majority of the inhabitants of the Arab Near East, remained
loyal to the Ottoman Government. They had no intention of
weakening "the only powerful Islamic Empire that remained."
Thus, the overworked phrase "Arab Awakening" was originally an
awakening to the abuses, the corruption and the despotism of the
Turkish regime and a desire to *reform* it, i.e., to put an end to
misgovernment, to grant the Arabs equal *rights* with the Turks
and a greater measure of political freedom and civil liberty. The
alternative of establishing an independent sovereign Arab Empire
as a result of separation from or extinction of the Ottoman Empire did not occur to the vast majority of the Muslims either as
desirable or as possible.

Arab demands for reforms were openly voiced after the
proclamation of the Constitution of 1876. The pages of one of
the earliest and much respected Arabic papers to appear in Beirut—the *Lisan al-Hal*—published by Khalil Sarkis, contained in
1878 many articles on the needed reforms in Lebanon and in the
Near East.[17] When 'Abdu'l Hamid appointed Midhat Pasha, the

"Father of Reform", as the *Vali* of Syria (1878-1880) there was great rejoicing in the country and hopes ran high that such reforms would be instituted.[18] But while the Christians of Lebanon wanted political reforms and political independence, the Muslim leaders sought not only reforms but to cleanse and to strengthen the Ottoman Empire by advocating a return to the purity of Islam and Muslim institutions, for the defense of the Muslim peoples against the West. They were all apostles of Pan-Islamism. The best known among them were Jamal-al-Din al-Afghani, Shaikh Muhammad 'Abdu, Muhammad Rashid Rida, the founder of the periodical *Al-Manar,* and 'Abd-al-Rahman al-Kawakibi. Jamal-al-Din maintained that unity among the Muslims was a natural and logical necessity. It was necessary for their protection, indeed for their very existence, in the face of Western imperialism. In 1884, joined by his friend and pupil, Muhammad 'Abdu, they began the publication of *Al-'Urwat al-Wuthqa*[19] (the Indissoluble Bond) "with the object of arousing the Muslim peoples to the need of uniting forces against Western aggression and exploitation",[20] Jamal-al-Din had made it very clear in his writings that his chief aim was "the unification of all Muslim peoples under one Islamic government, over which the one supreme Caliph should bear undisputed rule as in the glorious days of Islam..."[21]

Muhammad 'Abdu, called by H.A.R. Gibb "the greatest of the real reformers of Islam", wanted to free the mind from the fetters of traditions. He believed that "the disease" of the Muslims was in the first place their ignorance of their own religion, and secondly the despotism of their Muslim rulers.[22] His program included "the purification of Islam from corrupting influences and practices" and "the defense of Islam against European influences and Christian attacks".[23] Both Al-Afghani and Muhammad 'Abdu opposed European control of Muslim lands and "the pervasive influences of European culture and material civilization".

The fundamental character of Rashid Rida's reforms which he preached through the pages of his influential *Al-Manar,* followed the general line of his two predecessors: it was religious. He tried "to prove the suitability of Islam as a religious system... and the practicability of the Divine Law as an instrument of government". But it was first necessary to have "a thorough reform of the religion of Islam." The nationalists and political reformers in Egypt and Turkey were "atheists and infidels because religion is not fundamental to their ideas of nationality."[24]

As to Al-Kawakibi, he has left for us two remarkable books which describe his ideas and ideals for the revival of the Muslim world in general and the Arab world in particular: the *Umm al-Qura* and the *Taba'i' al-Istibdad*. Although his teachings about the regeneration of Islam and the unification of the world of Islam do not differ basically from all the exponents of Pan-Islamism, he "drew a sharp distinction between the Arab and the non-Arab Moslem peoples" and laid particular emphasis on "the special place to which Arabs were entitled in the fortunes of Islam by their language and by their descent."[25] Thus it is evident that among the leading Muslim thinkers and reformers of the nineteenth century in Egypt and Syria there was no anti-Turkish sentiment on national or racial grounds.

It must also be said in all fairness that the moderates among the Arab Christian writers and leaders of thought—although they despised and disliked the corrupt Turkish administrative machinery—did not wish to see the Ottoman Empire destroyed. Among them were such prominent men as Salîm Taqla, founder of the famous daily paper *Al-Ahram*, Faris Nimr Pasha, owner and editor of the equally famous *Al-Moqattam*, Jurji Zaidan, founder of the well-known periodical *Al-Hilâl*, Farah Antun, owner and editor of *Al-Jami'ah al-'Uthmaniyah* and the poet Khalil Mutran.

Towards the end of the nineteenth century, the internal situation began to deteriorate rapidly. Discontent, corruption and anarchy spread with alarming speed. The following two documents are significant. On August 24, 1888, the French Minister of Foreign Affairs wrote the following letter to M. Guillois, the French Consul in Damascus:

"Je vous remercie des indications que vous m'avez fait parvenir par votre rapport No. 21 au sujet de symptômes de mécontentement qui paraissent s'être manifestés depuis quelque temps parmi les officiers du Corps d'armée ottomane de la Syrie. Je n'ai pas lu sans inquiétude les passages de votre dépêche dans lesquels vous envisagez la possibilité d'un mouvement plus grave auquel prendrait part les populations arabes du Vilayet.

"Vous avez trop bien compris pour que j'ai besoin de vous le rappeler que le maintien de l'ordre dans cette partie de l'Empire ottoman est considéré par nous comme nécessaire à tous les points de vue..."[26]

The second document refers to the situation in Beirut and Damascus as "L'anarchie la plus complète", the words being those of M. de Petiteville, the French Consul General in Beirut to M. Flourens, the French Minister of Foreign Affairs. M. Petiteville wrote in his Despatch of January 11, 1888, from Beirut:

"... Il se trouve une foule de petits complots parmi les employés subalternes de l'ancien Vilayet. Le Mutessaref de Beyrouth est destitué, d'autres sont menacés d'un sort analogue, et ne pensent plus qu'à mettre en sûreté le pécule amassé aux dépens des administrés. En un mot, c'est l'anarchie la plus complète qui règne ici et à Damas."

And again in his Despatch of February 9, he stated:

"Ainsi que j'ai eu l'honneur de l'écrire précédemment à votre Excellence, l'anarchie règne ici — complète. Au sérail, le pouvoir est partagé entre trois hommes qui se le disputent : le Mutessaref d'une part que n'est pas sûr du lendemain, car il a été relevé de ses fonctions par la S. Porte; le cadi d'autre part — qui s'est arrogé un pouvoir discrétionnaire et enfin le Gouverneur militaire de la Place, Osman Pasha qui cherche à brimer l'autorité civile et qui trouve l'occasion opportune de frapper sur l'élément Chrétien."[27]

At the beginning of February 1894, M. Paul Cambon, the French Ambassador in Constantinople in his despatch to M.Casimir-Perrier, minister of Foreign Affairs, in connection with the Armenian Question, reported that the situation was not particular to Armenia, but that from one end of the Empire to the other the Greeks, the Albanians, the Arabs complained of lack of justice, of the corruption of Government officials and of the insecurity of life.[28]

At the turn of the century, when 'Abdu'l Hamid celebrated, on August 31, 1900, the twenty-fifth anniversary of his accession to the throne with great pomp and ceremony, Turkey's cup of iniquity was already overflowing. The die had been cast and the day of reckoning was approaching.

During the first years of the twentieth century, the existence of the "Arab Question" became known here and there in the Western world. *Le Réveil de la Nation Arabe* published in French by Negib 'Azoury, in 1905, clearly stated the aspirations and the goal of the extremists among the Arab nationalists. A strongly-worded manifesto addressed to the Great Powers by the "Arabian National Committee" said with much exaggeration and a great flight of imagination: "A great pacific change is on the eve of occurring in Turkey. The Arabs, whom the Turks tyrannized over only by keeping them divided on insignificant questions of ritual and religion, have become conscious of their national, historic, and racial homogeneity, and wish to detach themselves from the worm-eaten Ottoman trunk in order to form themselves into an independent State. This new Arab Empire will extend to its natural frontiers, from the valleys of the Tigris and Euphrates to the Isthmus of Suez, and from the Mediterranean to the Sea of Oman. It will be governed by the constitutional and liberal monarchy of an Arabian Sultan. The present Vilayet of the Hedjaz, together with the territory of Medina, will form an independent empire whose sovereign will be at the same time the religious Khaliph of all the Mohammedans. Thus one great difficulty, the separation of the civil and the religious powers in Islam, will have been solved for the greater good of all."[29]

But it was the Turks themselves who were planning and plotting to curb the autocratic powers of 'Abdu'l Hamid and bring to life again the suspended constitution of 1876. The "Young Turks", successors to the "New Ottomans" were stirred to action to save Turkey from utter disintegration and ruin. Much has been written about the genesis of the Young Turk movement.[30] The following account[31] is one of the best summaries about that movement:

"Driven underground by Abdu'l Hamid in the 'seventies, the Young Turkish movement sprang up again in the closing years of the century among the Turkish expatriates in Europe.

"In 1902 the first Young Turkish Congress met in Paris.[32] There and then the fundamentally nationalistic spirit of the old movement reasserted itself with redoubled vigor among the Turkish delegates, who now styled themselves the 'League of Union and Progress'.[33] In the face of the steady political and economic encroachments of the European Powers upon the independence of their Fatherland and in the face of the increasing separatist tendencies among the minorities in the Empire,[34] the L.U.P. gradually and inevitably assumed the leadership of the movement. By 1907, it succeeded in galvanizing the ranks of all the Young Turks for action. For the eventful years of 1905-08 gave this revolutionary movement a tremendous impetus. The relentless Macedonian Crusade, the naval demonstrations, the recrudescence of Russian activity in the Near East, the Anglo-Russian rapprochements, and the recurring rumors of dismemberment had terrified the Turkish patriots, who now came to regard the despot on the Golden Horn as the virtual prisoner of the 'Intriguing Powers'."

Consequently, in January 1907, the moderate wing of the Young Turks, the "Union Libérale" declared publicly for the principle of "The Ottoman Empire for the Ottomans" and demanded of Europe complete abstention from any further interference in Turkish Affairs. In December, the second Young Turkish Congress met in Paris under the leadership of the L.U.P. and adopted a "Declaration of Principles" that was clearly nationalistic, anti-European, and revolutionary. It openly advocated rebellion against the Sultan to save the Empire "from the venomous clutches of the greedy Powers," and projected a military uprising for the spring of 1909.[35]

The Young Turk movement had branches in different parts of the Ottoman Empire.[36] Egypt was one of the important centres of the Young Turk activities. Its distance from Constantinople, and particularly because it was under British administration, made the country a refuge for men with enlightened political ideas fearing the iron hand of 'Abdu'l Hamid. There is evidence that in 1899, a printing office was opened in Cairo by two members of the Young Turk party for the purpose of publishing a newspaper called "El Qanun el-Asasi" in the interests of their propaganda.[37]

But the nerve centre of the movement was the secret society of the Young Turks at Salonika, in Macedonia, where it "gained the allegiance of a considerable portion of that formidable Turkish army without whose co-operation, as the Christians in Macedonia knew well, no revolution had a chance of success."[38]

The July Revolution of 1908 put an end, temporarily, to the Hamidian regime.[39] 'Abdu'l Hamid acquiesced and on July 24, restored the Constitution of 1876. There was great rejoicing among Arabs and Turks, marked with parties, receptions and daily fêtes. The words "Liberty, Equality and Fraternity" were inscribed on Turkish banners. The Arabic literature of the time in Syria, Lebanon, Iraq and Egypt is full of panegyrics by the best poets about Sultan 'Abdu'l Hamid for grating a Constitution to the nation and thus putting an end to despotism and inaugurating an era of liberty, justice and equality.

The following eye-witness account of the reaction in Syria is worth recording here:

"On Sunday, P.M. July 26 (1908) as we were leaving the little 'Aleih chapel after the English service, Consul-General Ravendal startled us all with the telegraphic news that the Midhat Constitution of 1876, which had been suppressed by 'Abdu'l Hamid II for thirty two years, had now, July 23, been restored by a bloodless revolution effected by the Young Turkey Party...

"The whole empire burst forth in universal rejoicing, The press spoke out. Public meetings were held, cities and towns decorated; Moslems were seen embracing Christians and Jews, and inviting one another to receptions and feasts...The universal voice of the Moslems was, ... 'Now we are brethren and we can live in peace. We shall henceforth know each other only as Ottomans. Long live liberty! Long live the army! Long live the Sultan!'

"The pent-up feelings of the populace everywhere burst forth in loud hurrahs in the public streets. Syria has never seen such rejoicing. Can it be true? Will it last? were questions in all mouths. It was startling to those who had left Syria, early in July, under the old regime to be greeted in New York harbour with the news of free institutions in Turkey. It seemed too good to be true, and for weeks we here, foreigners and Syrians alike, seemed to be living in a dream. The Golden Age seemed to be dawning."[40]

The popularity of 'Abdu'l Hamid suddenly soared to a tremendous height.[41] The Illustrated London News of August 22, had a photograph of 'Abdu'l Hamid in his carriage at the first "Selamlik" after the granting of the Constitution, with the caption: "Once Abdu'l the Damned, now Abdu'l the Blessed: The Sultan's New Popularity."[42]

The first meeting of the new Parliament took place on Thursday December 17, 1908 in the presence of the Sultan and the Ottoman princes.[43] There was a total of 260 members, 119 of whom were Turks and 72 Arabs. By religions, 214 were Muslims, 42 Christians and 4 Jews. The Decentralization Party was represented by 35 members, the great majority of whom were non-Turks. Ahmad Rida Bey was elected President. The vice-presidents were a Greek, Aristidi Pasha, an Albanian, Nedchia Draga, and an Arab, Ruhi 'Abd al-Hadi. But 'Abdu'l Hamid, almost from the very first day, set about to get rid of the Young Turks, the Constitution and the New Parliament. On April 13, 1909, there was an attempt at a counter revolution in Istanbul.

However, the army in Macedonia, under the command of Shawkat Pasha, was ready. It immediately marched on the capital and laid siege to the Sultan's residence at Yildiz. The Parliament and the Senate met and voted the deposition of 'Abdu'l Hamid in favour of his brother, Muhammad Rashad, as Muhammad V.[44] Immediately afterwards, on the evening of April 27, 1909, 'Abdu'l Hamid accompanied by some members of his *Harem* and by a small retinue was exiled to Salonika and interned in Villa Alatini on the outskirts of the city.[45] Thus passed into history the last real Sultan of the Ottoman Empire, the last "Shadow of God" which fell upon a medieval and a legendary East—and with him ended the old destiny of the Turks which had been linked for nearly six hundred years with that of Asia and the peoples of Islam.

NOTES
AND REFERENCES

1. Pears, Sir Edwin, *Life of 'Abdu'l Hamid,* pp. 43 and 44. For a balanced evaluation of 'Abdu'l Hamid and his foreign policy, see Professor A. Vambéry's article on "Personal Recollections of 'Abdu'l Hamid II and His Court" in *The Nineteenth Century and After* for June and July, 1909. The mother of Sultan 'Abdu'l Hamid was Tirimüjgân (Kadin Efendi) who died when he was still a very young child.

2. France — *Archives du Ministère des Affaires Etrangères, Turquie,* vol. 423 for December 1878.

3. "In the early years of 'Abdu'l Hamid, the chief mosques in Stamboul contained extracts from the Sacred Books of the qualifications required in the Caliph. About 1890, by 'Abdu'l Hamid's command, these were ordered to be taken down, and a considerable amount of discontent was thus created amongst the Ulama..." Pears, p. 149.

4. "Arabs and Circassians were always preferred by him as more faithful and more humble than the Turks; hence his predilection for Izzet Ebul-Huda and Emin Efendi." Professor A. Vambéry, "Personal Recollections of 'Abdul Hamid II and His Court" in *The Nineteenth Century and After,* July 1909, p. 989.

5. To mention only a few: 'Izzat Pasha al-'Abid, "contemptuously called by the Turks 'Arab Izzet'", was the Second Secretary of 'Abdu'l Hamid; Na'um Pasha "The Syrian" was Under Secretary for Foreign Affairs; Salim Pasha Melhamah, a Maronite from Lebanon, was Minister of Mines, Forests and Agriculture; Najib Pasha Melhamah (brother of the former) was entrusted with the safety of the Sultan— "Gidiç Mémuru". (His official position was Under-Secretary at the Ministry of Public Works but he was actually the unofficial Head of the Secret Police and Special Political Envoy of the Sultan). Mahmud Shawkat Pasha (from a well-known family in Iraq) was Commander-in-chief of the Third Army at Salonika, which marched on Constantinople and deposed 'Abdu'l Hamid. See Gooch, and Temperley, vol. V, pp. 7-20; and Al-A'zami, Ahmad 'Izzat, *Al-Qadiyah al-'Arabiyah,* pp. 80-82.

6. Great Britain, *Handbook* No. 96a and b, *The Rise of Islam and the Caliphate; The Pan-Islamic Movement,* pp. 54-55.

7. Cited by *The Illustrated London News* of October 10, 1908, (No. 3625, vol. CXXXIII), p. 498.
    "Externally, he ('Abdu'l Hamid) was very popular among the Muslims of other countries. Very shrewdly, he saw that England and France, the two countries with the largest number of Moslem subjects, would naturally be affected by Pan-Islamism. The building of the Hejaz railway was a masterly demonstration of his Pan-Islamism."— Edib, Halidé, *Turkey Faces West,* (New Haven, 1930) p. 93.

8. Al-Maqdisi, Ruhi Khalidi, *Al-Inqilab al-'Uthmani wa Turkiya al-*

Fatat, cited in "Al-Hilal", vol. 17, Part III (December 1, 1908), p. 139. However, the debates which took place in that Parliament and which have been discovered and published recently, seem to indicate that its subservience to Abdu'l Hamid has been greatly exaggerated. See Us, Hakki Tarik, *Meclis-i-Meb'usan, 1293-1877,* 2 vols. (Istanbul 1954).

9. Gallenga, the correspondent of the *Times* at Constantinople reported on June 21, 1876 that to create constitutional government in Turkey was "something like weaving ropes of sand." Cited in Seton-Watson, R.W., *Disraeli, Gladstone and the Eastern Question* (London, 1935), p. 38.

10. After the British occupation of Egypt in 1882, Arab and Turkish nationalists flocked to Cairo and Alexandria where they enjoyed great freedom for their political activities. Sometime soon after 1897, the first political society founded by Arab leaders in Egypt appeared under the name of *Jam'iyat al-Shawra al-'Uthmani* (the Ottoman Consultative Society). Two of its founders were Muhammad Rashid Rida and Rafiq al-'Azim. But other nationals in the Ottoman Empire took part in its organization and its activities such as Turks, Armenians and Circassians. The purpose of the organization was to oppose 'Abdu'l Hamid's tyranny and unjust administration and to try to change the form of Government into a representative Parliamentary system. 'Abdu'l Hamid was, naturally, greatly perturbed by it. He himself confessed to one of his entourage that when he first heard about that Society, he could not sleep for three nights until he learned, through some of his spies in Egypt, as to who its founders were. He called it the "corrupting society".

The *Jam'iyat al-Shawra al-'Uthmani* had several branches throughout the Empire. Its propaganda material was printed in Arabic and Turkish. Some of it used to be sent with passengers and members of the crew of Russian ships to Turkish ports on the Black Sea. From there, secret messengers would take them and distribute them throughout Anatolia.

The society dissolved itself soon after the Young Turks came to power in 1908.—See Al-'Azm *Majmu'at Athar Rafiq Bey al-'Azm,* part 1.

Some years later, René Pinon wrote: "l'Egypte devient... le centre d'une véritable renaissance de la vie et de la civilisation arabe, par la langue, par la littérature, par la religion. Il est donc naturel de supposer que la propagande nationale arabe et la publicité qui lui a été donnée dans l'Europe occidentale, loin d'être des phénomènes isolés, sont en connexion étroite avec le grand mouvement d'indépendance qui se manifeste dans l'Arabie péninsulaire et dont l'Angleterre a si ouvertement favorisé le succès"— Pinon, R., *l'Europe et l'Empire Ottoman,* (Paris, 1908) p. 382.

11. Thanks to the existence of foreign Post offices in Asiatic possessions of the Ottoman Empire, the liberals and the anti-Turks could keep in touch with one another. All communications passing through these Post Offices were safe from 'Abdu'l Hamid's spies and censors—

except in certain cases when some employee would be tempted with a large sum of money to "sell" to 'Abdu'l Hamid certain important letters.

12. Antonius, p. 79.

13. Faris Nimr Pasha was born in Lebanon, in the village of Hasbaya, most probably in 1854. He left Beirut for Cairo in 1885 where he, together with Ya'qub Sarruf and Shahin Makarius, founded in 1886 the Arabic daily paper called "Al-Mokattam", one of the most famous newspapers, in the Arab world. Faris Nimr Pasha died in 1951.

14. The following were some of the prominent members: Ibrahim al-Hourani, Ya'qub Sarruf, Ibrahim al-Yaziji, Faris Nimr Pasha and Shahin Makarius.

   According to Faris Nimr Pasha, the group consisted at first of about twelve members, increasing later to nearly seventy. He told the author about the great influence of a certain Elias Habbalin who taught French at the Syrian Protestant College in Beirut from 1871-1874. He was a Maronite then he poined the Freemasons. He had read Voltaire and was very progressive and revolutionary in his ideas. After going briefly over the French lesson in his class, Habbalin would turn to politics and talk about getting rid of the Turks with all their injustices and corrupt Government. His students, all of whom were Christians, soon became his enthusiastic disciples. Every one of them wanted to become a Habbalin "and more than a Habbalin". They started to teach their ideas to others. Another young enthusiast was Salim 'Ammun from Dair-al-Qamar. His uncle had been the Governor of Lebanon in the days of Ibrahim Pasha. He had read Dumas', *Three Musketeers,* and together with two other friends of his tried to become like the three Musketeers and form a secret Society to free Lebanon from the Turks. According to Nimr Pasha, the first revolutionary ideas which he and a group of his friends got while at the Syrian Protestant College, were of French origin and came to them secretly through Elias Habbalin.

15. This society was responsible for the anonymous placards which denounced the evils of Turkish misgovernment and exhorted the population to overthrow it. These placards were stuck, after midnight, on walls near Consulates of Foreign Powers, in Beirut, Damascus and Tripoli. Faris Nimr Pasha told the author that many of them were in his own handwriting.

   For an exaggerated account of the importance of this society and of its placards, see Antonius, pp. 79-86.

16. It is not possible to give an exact date but sometime between 1882 and 1883, the "secret revolutionary society" suspended its activities, burned its records, and dissolved itself.

17. See issues of *Lisan al-Hal* No. 92 of September 14, 1878 and No. 117 of December 11/27, 1878, This paper is still being published in Beirut.

18. See *Lisan al-Hal*, No. 109 of November 25, 1878 and No. 112 of December 5, 1878.

19. *Al-'Urwat al-Wuthqa* was also the name of a secret society founded by Jamal-al-Din and composed of Muslims of India, Egypt, North Africa and Syria, the purpose of which was "to unite the Muslims, arouse them from their sleep, acquaint them with the dangers threatening them and guide them to the way of meeting and overcoming those dangers."—*Al-Manar*, vol. VIII (August 17, 1905) p. 55.

20. See Adams, Charles, *Islam and Modernism in Egypt*, pp. 1-13.

21. *Ibid.*, p. 13.

22. See *Al-Manar*, vol. VIII, part 12 (August 17, 1906) p. 465 and part 23, (January 26, 1906) p. 893.

23. Gibb, H.A.R., *Modern Trends in Islam*, p. 33.

24. See Adams, pp. 181-187.

25. See Antonius, pp. 95-98.

26. France, *Archives du Ministère des Affaires Etrangères, Turquie* vol. 14, *Damas* — 1855-1888.

27. France, — *Archives du Ministères des Affaires Etrangères, Turquie, Beyrouth*, 1888.

28. See Contenson, p. 3.
"The state of the Law Courts is worse than it ever was before, and complaints of want of justice are continually being made." Great Britain—F.O. 195/1365—*"State of Affairs in Syria"*, Despatch No. 46, dated "Beyrout, October 5, 1881" See also F.O. 195/1306, Despatch dated "Damascus, February 10, 1880", and F.O. 195/1369, Despatch No. 60, dated "Beyrout, December 19, 1881."

29. English translation, in Stoddard, L., *The new World of Islam*, p. 171. For the original French text, see 'Azoury, Negib, *Le Réveil de la Nation Arabe*, pp. I-IV.

30. See Gooch, and Temperley, vol. V, *The Near East, 1903-9*, pp. 248-262 and 272-307; David, Wade Dewood, *European Diplomacy in the Near Eastern Question, 1906-1909*, pp. 60-61; Mears, E. G., *Modern Turkey*, pp. 476-490; Knight, E. F., *The Awakening of Turkey*, pp. 70-94 and Zaydan, G., *Al-Hilal*, vol. XVII (1908) pp. 3-31. See also Tunaya, Tarik Z., *Türkiyede Siyasi Partilar, 1859-1952* (Istanbul, 1952) pp. 91.

31. See David, pp. 60-61. See also Ramsaur, pp. 52-95.

32. "As the result of differences on the method to be pursued, the delegates to the Congress split into two factions. The Turkish delegates bolted and organized the 'League of Union and Progress' while the rest, composed of representatives of the disaffected minorities, organ-

ized themselves as the 'League of Private Initiative and Decentralization' (better known as the *Union Libérale)* under the leadership of
Prince Sabahiddin, the exiled nephew of Abdulhamid. The former
(L.U.P.) advocated the transformation of the whole State system into
a compact unit in order to save the Empire from dismemberment ;
the latter *(Union Libérale)* proposed to achieve the same end through
decentralization, a system of communal and religious particularism.
See Ahmed Niyazi, *Khawatir Niyazi,* p. 29 ; *Al-Manar,* XI, p. 852
ff. ; Ismail Kemal, *The Memoirs of Ismail Kemal Bey* (London, 1920)
pp. 306-8 ; G. Hanotaux, *La Politique de l'Equilibre, 1907-1911,* pp.
135-6, 139 ; A. Hamilton, *Problems of the Middle East* (London,
1909) pp. 11-13 ; D. von Mikusch, *Gasi Mustafa Kemal,* pp. 43-5."
—*Ibid.,* p. 60, n. 4.

33. "The term 'Young Turks' denotes the body of reformers within the
Ottoman Empire, while the term 'League of Union and Progress'
usually abbreviated into L.U.P., designates the organization of Turk-
ish liberals that became the driving power behind the Revolution.
Likewise, the term 'Central Committee of Union and Progress,' more
frequently designated as C.U.P., refers to the inner circle of The
L.U.P. Up to the autumn of 1908, there were several C.U.P.'s or
'Committees.' "—*Ibid.,* p. 60 n. 5.

34. "The L.U.P. published in Paris an official organ, *Meshveret,* through
which it propagated revolutionary ideas. Its distinctly nationalistic
and anti-European tone drew the admiration of Abdulhamid himself.
Tahsin Pasha, *Abdulhamid ve Yildiz Hatiralari* (Istanbul, 1921) p.
295. Cf. Driault et l'Héritier, *Histoire diplomatique de la Grèce,* V.
2-3."—*Ibid.,* pp. 60-61, n. 6. See also Ramsaur, pp. 23-37.

35. In addition to the Young Turks Committee, there were other non-
Muslim and non-Turkish revolutionary Committees: "En 1907 les
groupes arméniens, macédonians, bulgares, serbes, grecs, bosniaques
et herzégoviniens se réunirent de nouveau à Genève et exprimèrent le
vœu de voir proclamer l'autonomie de la Macédonie, de l'Arménie,
de l'Albanie, de la Bosnie et de l'Herzégovine, formant ensemble une
Confédération Balkanique avec une constitution unique pour tous, y
compris les Turcs. Ces idées flottaient dans l'air, elles échauffaient
l'âme de tous les chrétiens d'Orient."—Djuvara, T. G., *Cent Projets
de Partage de la Turquie (1281-1913),* (Paris, 1914) p. 503, citing *Le
Journal de Genève du 15 février 1907.* Djuvara adds: "Vers la même
époque, à la fin de l'année 1905, le Prince Sabeheddine adressa aux
Chancelleries un Mémoire qui finissait par ce cri patriotique 'L'Empire
ottoman aux Ottomans'. C'était la devise de la *Turquie Libérale,* qui
devait assurer 'la paix universelle'. C'était vraiment trop beau ; six
ans après, nous eûmes la mêlée balkanique".

36. Of the centres outside Turkey, Paris and Geneva were the most important. In Geneva, the Young Turks published a paper called *The
Osmanli.* In the first issue of its English Supplement dated July 15,
1898, they wrote: "We desire that this publication should be as far
as possible the organ of the legitimate claims of all Ottoman subjects

irrespective of race and religion, and our demand is for those reforms needed not only in this or that part of the empire but in the empire as a whole..."

At the end of the paper there is an article attacking 'Abdu'l Hamid in violent language: "Of all the Sultans who have reigned over Turkey, Abdu'l Hamid is the sole figure essentially abject."

37. Great Britain, London, F.O., See *Further Correspondence Respecting the Affairs of Egypt, 1902,* Part LX, Documents 44, p. 114 ; and 50, pp. 116-9: The Earl of Cromer to the Marquess of Lansdowne, dated Cairo April 11 and 14, 1902.

38. Knight, p. 93.

39. It may be of interest to state that one of the modern means of communication, the telegraph, recently introduced in Turkey, played an important rôle in the success of the Revolution. The orders which the Sultan sent telegraphically from Yildiz against the C.U.P. became immediately known to the Committee because it had among its members "most of the telegraph and railway employees". Tal'at, one of the principal leaders of the Revolution was the secretary-general of the Telegraph Bureau at Monastir. 'Abdu'l Hamid himself was threatened telegraphically that if he did not restore the Constitution of 1876, the army of Salonika would march on Constantinople.

40. Jessup, Henry Harris, *Fifty-three Years in Syria,* vol. II, pp. 785-787.
The official British Extract from the Annual Report for Turkey for the year 1908 says: "It would hardly be possible to find a more violent contrast than that between the Reports on Syria which reached this Embassy up to the end of July and those sent during the remainder of the year.

"For the first seven months one finds nothing but complaints of every kind of injustice, venality, and corruption, from the Vali (the chief offender of all) downwards. Public security hardly existed. Smuggling was rampant, carried on as it was under a well-organized system.

"Nazim Pasha, after only four months of office, has succeeded in keeping an effective control on the various Government Departments, and in improving the efficiency of the police and gendarmerie, with the result that the administration of the vilayet has been satisfactory, order has been maintained, and the flourishing business in contraband of arms, tobacco, and tombac stopped, and this without recourse having been had to the military authorities."—Gooch, and Temperley, vol. V, p. 303.

41. "At one time, the unpopularity of the Sultan was such that he ceased to attend the ordinary Friday prayers—the ceremony known as Selamlik at the Hamidie Mosque. Since the granting of the Constitution all that is changed, and the Sultan's guard have now to protect him from the enthusiasm of his people..."—*The Illustrated London News,* August 22, 1908, p. 264.

42. *Ibid.*

43. For an account of the Revolution of 1908, the meeting of the new

Parliament and the speech of 'Abdu'l Hamid at the opening of Parliament, see Stitt, George, *A Prince of Arabia,* pp. 95-101— "Hunched and haggard, he (Sultan 'Abdu'l Hamid) shuffled slowly to the Imperial Box and gazed down upon the House, looking pale and nervous. All rose and saluted. Abdu'l Hamid replied, and then signed to his First Secretary to read the speech from the throne..." Among other things, Abdu'l Hamid said: "...The intellectual progress of the people having reached the desired standard, we have acquired the conviction that Parliament should once more assemble as a guarantee of the present and future prosperity of our country... Our resolution to govern the country in conformity with the Law of the Constitution is irrevocable (cheers). May it please the Almighty to grant that your endeavours shall be crowned with success and that our Fatherland shall enjoy every blessing. God aid us in our task."— *Ibid.,* pp. 99-101.

44. The Shaikh al-Islam supported the decision by a *fatwa* based on the Shari'a law.

45. He had requested to be allowed to spend the rest of his life in the Cheraghan Palace, on the European shore of the Bosphorus. But this request was refused. In 1912 he was transferred back to Constantinople to the Palace of Beylerbey on the Bosphorus, where he died on February 10, 1918.

CHAPTER V

THE EMERGENCE OF ARAB NATIONALISM

Part 1 — Under the Young Turks
1909 - 1914

We have seen in the previous two chapters that although the Arabs had many grievances against the Turkish Government, they—with the exception of the Maronites of Lebanon and the Wahhabis of Arabia—entertained no idea of separation from the Ottoman Empire. Their main emphasis was on *reforms*. And even when they severely criticized the Sultanate, they remained loyal to the Caliphate. However, at the beginning of the twentieth century between 1908 and 1918 when the Young Turks were in power, Arab-Turkish relations suffered a great strain and underwent a marked change. The Arabs continued to ask for reforms but the main object of these reforms was Arab autonomy in their own Provinces and within the framework of the Ottoman Empire. The establishment of complete Arab independence and Arab national sovereignty was an after-thought.

"The Young Turk revolution of 1908 promised equality to all Ottoman subjects without distinction of religion and race. These promises, however, were never carried out."[1] This failure made the break between the Arabs and Turks inevitable.[2] Thus the years 1908 and more especially 1909 were decisive years in the destiny of the Ottoman Empire.[3]

There is no evidence that the Young Turks came to power with the avowed intention of ignoring Islam and the non-Turkish elements in the Ottoman Empire and of embarking on a policy of Turkification. An official and authoritative publication has given the following clear summary of the situation: "The Committee of Union and Progress were not Nationalists to begin with, chiefly because they ignored the nationality problems of the Ottoman Empire. Their primary aim was to maintain the integrity of the Empire, especially in Europe; and in this they agreed with 'Abdu'l Hamid and all previous rulers of Turkey. They only differed as to the means, for, while 'Abdu'l Hamid believed in despotism at home and a balance of jealousy among the European Powers, the Committee of Union and Progress held that Turkey's best safeguard was internal strength, and the best source of strength, political liberty. Their ideas of liberty were drawn from the French Revolution. 'Liberty, Equality, and Fraternity' would be proclaimed; all inhabitants of the Empire would rally to the State as free Ottoman citizens, just as Picards and Marseillais and Alsatians rallied to the French Republic after 1789; and the question of Nationality would solve itself.

"This actually happened during the first six weeks after the proclamation of the Constitution in 1908. Men of all creeds and races embraced each other in the streets. But, then, they drew apart again and considered how they might turn the new regime to their own advantage. The Balkan nationalities rejected the offer of a liberal Turkey altogether, and determined to take the first opportunity of completing their own unity and independence at Turkey's expense. Others, like the Arabs, the Armenians and the Constantinopolitan and Anatolian Greeks, recognized that secession was impossible, but took measures to defend their own national individuality within the Ottoman State. The Arabs formed the main opposition in the new Parliament...The Committee of Union and Progress found that the Turks were the only element in the Empire that was not opposed to centralization and had no political ideal incompatible with the Ottoman State idea. They therefore fell back upon their Turkish nationality, and came to think of Turkification as the natural means of achieving their ends..."[4]

It was not only towards the Arabs that they failed to pursue their cardinal policy of equal treatment for all races in their Empire, but the Young Turks showed equal, if not more, intransigence towards their Christian subjects in the Balkans. On August 28, 1910, Mr. A. Geary, the British Acting Consul at Monastir, wrote to Sir G. Lowther, the British Ambassador in Constantinople: "I have the honour to report to your Excellency that I have obtained from a confidential source the substance of the speech recently made at Salonica by Talaat Bey to the members of the local Committee of Union and Progress, assembled in secret conclave and am now informed that Djavid Bey's speech made in similar circumstances at Monastir substantially followed the same train of thought".

In this speech, Talaat Bey is reported to have said:

"You are aware that by the terms of the Constitution equality of Mussulman and Ghiaur was affirmed but you, one and all, know and feel that this is an unrealizable ideal. The Sheriat, our whole past history and the sentiments of hundreds of thousands of Mussulmans and even the sentiments of the Ghiaurs themselves, who stubbornly resist every attempt to Ottomanize them, present an impenetrable barrier to the establishment of real equality. We have made unsuccessful attempts to convert the Ghiaur into loyal Osmanli and all such efforts must inevitably fail, as long as the small independent States in the Balkan Peninsula remain in a position to propagate ideas of Separatism among the inhabitants of Macedonia. There can therefore be no question of equality, until we have succeeded in our task of Ottomanizing the Empire—a long and laborious task, in which I venture to predict that we shall at length succeed after we have at last put an end to the agitation and propaganda of the Balkan States."[5]

Nine days later on September 6, Sir G. Lowther wrote to Sir Edward Grey: "That the Committee have given up any idea of Ottomanizing all the non-Turkish elements by sympathetic and constitutional ways has long been manifest. To them 'Ottoman' evidently means 'Turk' and their present policy of 'Ottomanization' is one of pounding the non-Turkish elements in a Turkish mortar. It was hoped that perhaps as they became more firmly seated in the saddle and effective opposition had disappeared under the pressure of the state of siege, the Committee would broaden rather than narrow their policy as regards internal administration but Talaat Bey's utterances seem to make the fulfilment of such hopes more remote."[6]

Between 1908 and 1911, the Young Turks believed that their Constitution could do away with Pan-Islamism. "We Ottomans

belong to a race sufficiently intelligent and practical to understand that the pursuit of the Pan-Islamic designs of the visionaries
would be contrary to our dearest interests."[7] But the leaders of
the revolution soon realized that the binding force of Pan-Islamism
was much stronger than they had anticipated and it seems almost
certain that "by the year 1911, the Committee of Union and Progress had definitely adopted the Pan-Islamic programme, in their
foreign policy, at any rate."[8] On December 27, 1911, *The Times*
reported that the following decisions were among those arrived
at by the Salonika Congress (1911) of the Committee of Union
and Progress:

"A Congress of delegates, summoned from all the Moslem
countries of the world, ought to meet annually in Constantinople,
to discuss questions of interest to the Moslem world. Branches
of the Committee should be formed in all Moslem countries, especially in Russia and in Persia. The Mohammedans of Russia
ought to be persuaded to make revolutionary propaganda among
Russian soldiers..."[9] It has even been asserted that side by side
with the Committee of Union and Progress, there was a great Pan-
Islamic league, called *"Jam'iyyet Hairiyyeh Hamiyyeh"*, the last
meeting of which "was attended by five Indians".[10]

"Declarations that any real toleration by Islam of other religions and any progress of the Moslem world in the direction of
European civilization were impossible are quoted by a collabo-
rator of Sherif Pasha from the writings of a member of both these
bodies, the Sheikh 'Abd al-Haqq of Baghdad; and apparently the
Comtist Ahmad Riza, first President of the Ottoman Chamber
of the Deputies, came round to the view that the Moslem religion
was the only force capable of uniting the different elements of
the Ottoman Empire...It was the duty (he held) of all Moslems to
labour to maintain the integrity of the Ottoman Empire."[11] A Society calling itself The Progress of Islam *("Endjoman-i Terekki—
Islam")* was founded in Geneva. It published (in French) its first
Bulletin, in February 1913, in which it stated its purpose to be
the strengthening of the ties between the divers Muslim nations
and to help in their intellectual and economic progress". It made
it clear that it championed the cause of Islam, defended the regime in Turkey and was at the same time violently anti-British

and anti-French. A sheet in Arabic enclosed in that Bulletin speaks in glowing terms of the glories of Islam, glories which had now departed and concludes that it is now the duty of every Muslim to rise to the assistance of "the country of the Caliphate" (Turkey) which was "the last refuge of Islam."[12]

But the Arab Muslim leaders doubted the sincerity of the Committee of Union and Progress, mainly for two reasons: "In the first place, the leaders of that Committee (were) without exception, Freemasons; and such religious fanaticism conflicts with the principles of the Masonic Society"[13] and, secondly, "the Salonika Jews (were) inseparable from the Committee of Union and Progress".[14] Seton-Watson wrote: "The main fact about the Committee of Union and Progress is its essentially un-Turkish and un-Moslem character. From the very first hardly one among its true leaders has been a pure-blooded Turk. Enver is the son of a renegade Pole. Djavid belongs to the Jewish sect of Dunmehs. Carasso is a Sephardim Jew from Salonica. Talaat is an Islamised Bulgarian gypsy. Achmet Riza, one of the group's temporary figureheads, is half Circassian and half Magyar, and a Positivist of the school of Comte."[15] Soon Arab doubts were substantiated and the newly born Turkish nationalism of a most chauvinistic type asserted itself and clashed with the Arabs' pride in their race, religion and language. One can rightly say that the seeds of Arab separatist movement began to sprout from the soil of Turkish nationalism from 1909 onwards. This expression of Turkish nationalism has been called "Pan-Turanianism—a supernational propaganda for a rapprochement between all the Turkish-speaking peoples, on the same lines as Pan-Slavism".[16] Perhaps the best exposition of this doctrine is found in *Turkismus und Panturkismus* of Tekin Alp,[17] published in Weimar in 1915, in the writings of Yusuf Bey Akçuraoglu[18] and Ziya Bey Gökalp[19] and in two Turkish books: *Qawm Jadid* (A New Nation)[20] containing the sermons delivered by 'Ubaidullah, a Shaikh of Afghani origin, in the mosque of Aya Sofia, and *Ta'rikh al-Mustaqbal* (A History of the Future), by the well-known Turkish writer Jalal Nuri Bey. All these works stirred the Turks for a national regeneration on "Pure Turkish" lines based on the natural affinities of all Turkish-speaking peoples. "The moral drawn by the Young Turks was that return to their pre-Islamic institutions would bring national rejuvenation and at the same time would provide a basis for cooperation with other Turkish-speaking peoples outside the Ottoman frontiers."[21]

At first, the Committee of Union and Progress seems to have decided to exploit both Pan-Islamism and Pan-Turanianism, at the same time, the former, principally in their Muslim territories outside Anatolia proper and the latter, at home. But there is little doubt that at heart the Committee made Pan-Turanianism their main objective.

The following excellent summary of the anti-Islamic and anti-Arab policy of the Young Turks will be recorded here in full in order to understand clearly, by contrast, the anti-Turkish reaction which that policy created among the Arabs, a reaction which had a disastrous result for the Ottoman Empire:

"(a) Ziya Bey's group first came into conflict with Islam over the language question. They probably thought of translating the Koran, etc., into Turkish because they knew that the translation of the Bible and Christian liturgy into English and German at the Protestant Reformation had been the foundation of the modern English and German national literature. The idea is not intrinsically contrary to the Muhammadan religion; but it is distinctly contrary to Islamic prejudice, and has therefore not been taken up by the Committee of Union and Progress.

"(b) The opposition of the Moslem ecclesiastics to the translation of the Koran into Turkish led the Turkish Nationalists into an attack on Islam as an ecclesiastical institution. This secularist movement, too, is partly an imitation of Europe, as 'Takin Alp's' use of the word 'clericals' shows; but it also embodies sound and necessary reforms like the secularization of Education and the Law, and steps in this direction have been taken by the Committee of Union and Progress themselves. The chief difference on this head between the Committee of Union and Progress and the doctrinaires is that, while the latter trumpet their 'anti-clericalism', the Committee of Union and Progress try to carry secularization through with as little friction as possible, and without ever admitting that their measures are anti-Islamic.

"(c) The Nationalists have also started a 'pre-Islamic' movement which is only paralleled in Europe by the 'Ur-Deutschtum' of the Hindenburg wooden idols. They are making a sentimental cult of the pagan Turanian conquerors, like Jenghis Khan and Hulaku (both of whom, incidentally, were Mongols and not Turks). Members of the 'Turk Kuji' ("Turkish Power") Society—an association for the promotion of Physical culture, probably modelled on the Slavonic 'Sokols'—have to take 'Turanian' club-names in place of Moslem (e.g. 'Oghus' for 'Muhammad'); and a corps of Turkish Boyscouts has been instituted, who likewise take 'Turanian' scout-names, cheer for the 'Khakan of the Turks' instead of the 'Padishah', and carry flags with the Turkish wolf on them though the representation of living creatures in art is tabu to good Moslems.

"Enver was said to be the patron of these boy-scouts; a Turkish army order came into the hands of the British War Office directing the troops to include the 'Grey Wolf' in their prayers; and the Turanian idea seems to have made a certain progress among individual Turks of distinction, even in this fantastic form. For instance, King Hussein's troops captured, on the corpse of a brother of the Turkish Commandant at Medina, a circular issued by the principal Pan-Turanian Society in Turkey, the 'Turk Ojagi' ('The Turkish Hearth'), in which the following passage occurs:

" 'That monstrous figment of imagination which is known as the Community of Islam, and which has for long past stood in the way of present progress generally, and of the realization of the principles of Turanian Unity in particular, has now entered on a phase of decline and ruin. We need not apprehend from it any further danger to the execution of our hopes and principles. This is abundantly shown by the state of affairs among the Moslems in India...'

"This circular derives a certain importance from its source and ownership, but there is no evidence that the 'Back to Paganism' movement has any influence over the policy of the Committee of Union and Progress."[22]

As a result of the Young Turks' Turkifying program, the

Arab leaders' objective of gaining full national independence received a great stimulus which consolidated it. As far as Arab political nationalism is concerned, it can safely be asserted that it was the national and racial policy of the Young Turks which fanned its flames. Nationalist sentiments are dangerous to play with in a multi-racial and multi-national empire. A nationalist revival is bound to generate so much rivalry and antagonism as to lead inevitably to the break up of such an empire. Hence, when the Young Turks made the nationalist ideal and their racial superiority the basis of a new Turkey, culturally and politically united and strong, the Arab leaders' reaction was to think precisely in the same terms about the future of the Arab lands. As a result, a number of Arab societies and political parties were formed by enlightened and educated young Arabs to defend the Arab cause and protect the Arab rights[23] among which were the following, established after 1908: (1) *Jam'iyat al-Ikha' al'Arabi al-'Uthmani* (The Society of Arab Ottoman Brotherhood); (2) *Al-Muntada al-Adabi* (The Literary Club); (3) *Al-Jam'iyat al-Qahtaniyah* (The Qahtani Society)[24]; (4) *Al-'Alam al-Akhdar* (The Green Flag); (5) *Al-'Ahd* (The Covenant), all of which were founded in Constantinople, and (6) *Jam'iyat Beirut al-Islamiyah* (The Reform Society of Beirut); (7) *Jam'iyat Basrah al-Islamiyah* (The Reform Society of Basrah); (8) *Al-Nadi al-Watani al-'Ilmi* (The National Literary Club) founded in Baghdad and finally the two most important organizations: (9) *Jam'iyat al-'Arabiyah al-Fatat,* better known simply as *Al-Fatat* (The Young Arab Society) and (10) *Hizb al-Lamarkaziyah al-Idariyah al-'Uthmani* (The Ottoman Administrative Decentralization Party).[25] It is not, however, the purpose of this chapter to give an account of all these societies but to dwell briefly on two of them: *Al-Fatat* and the *Hizb al-Lamarkaziah.*

Al-Fatat was an ultra secret Arab society of which it has been written: "No other society had played as determining a part in the history of the national movement,"[26] while the Decentralization Party was, on the other hand, a public political party which became "the best organized and most authoritative spokesman of Arab aspirations."[27]

The *Fatat* society was founded in Paris on November 14,

1909 by a group of Arab students who were then pursuing their higher studies in that city, most active among whom was Tawfiq al-Natur.[28] It is significant that this society was an entirely Muslim Arab organization. It was first called *Jam'iyat al-Natiqin bi'l Dad*[29] which was later, in 1911, changed to *Al-Jam'iyat al-'Arabiyah Al-Fatat*. The purpose of the society was, politically, to obtain Arab independence within the framework of a bi-racial Ottoman Empire, Arab and Turk, on lines similar to the Austro-Hungarian Empire. In addition, the society's aim was to raise the Arab *"Umma"* to the level of the social and educational advance made by the Western nations. But all this was to be done without breaking down the unity or destroying the existence of the Ottoman Empire itself.[30] Halidé Edib herself, in her criticism of the Young Turks' policy, admits that "the reduced empire" could not be strong enough "to resist the overwhelming forces arrayed against it" except through "a close understanding between the Turks and the Arabs." She says further: "It is true that the Arabs were already seized with the nationalist fever, but there was an idea ascribed to Mahmoud Shevket Pasha, himself of Arab origin, which was worth a trial. It was the creation of a dual monarchy, Arabo-Turkish, with the seat of government at Aleppo. Whether it could have prevented Moslem disintegration or not, one cannot be certain but the experiment should have been made."[31] Ziya Gökalp who is "regarded by many as the spiritual father of Turkish nationalism and as one of the outstanding Turkish thinkers in modern times" hoped at one time that the non-Turkish nationalities in the Ottoman Empire could live side by side in cooperation and agreement with the Turks. "Shortly before the outbreak of the First World War he suggested the establishment of a bi-national State (to be called the Turco-Arab State) under the Ottoman Caliph...In 1918, he proposed a federation or confederation of two independent States, Turkish Anatolia and 'Arabistan'. This union, he said, was natural for geographical as well as religious reasons and vital for the defense of both nations. It would be beneficial especially for the Arabs who, lacking civil and military organization, would be conquered by European powers as soon as they separated themselves from their Turkish brothers."[32] However, the defeat of the Ottoman

Empire and the loss of all the Arab provinces put an end to all such possibilities.

"The idea of Arab nationalism—or 'Arabism'—was not yet strong in us", the late Tawfiq al-Natur, told the author. "All that we, as Arabs, wanted was to have the same rights and obligations in the Ottoman Empire, as the Turks themselves and to have the Empire composed of two great nationalities: the Turks and the Arabs".[33] This same desire of unity in diversity was brought out in the political program of the Turkish party of *Hurriyet wa E'telaf* (Freedom and Unity). This party was based on one of the two currents of thought prevalent in the new Turkish Parliament of 1908: administrative decentralization of the Ottoman Empire as against the highly centralized policy of the Party of Union and Progress. Apparently, it was Prince Sabah-al-Din, the son of Damad Mahmud Pasha and nephew of Sultan 'Abdu'l Hamid who first supported and promoted the idea of political decentralization: *'adem-i-Merkeziyet*. He, his brother Lutfullah and their father had escaped to France during the height of the Hamidian despotism, in 1899. He was very popular with the Turkish Liberals, the *Ahrar*, whom he encouraged and directed, and with all non-Turkish elements in the Empire. He gathered together in Paris about forty-seven Ottoman liberals composed of all races and religions in the Empire—including Arabs—and encouraged them to remain united under the name of Ottoman.[34] Returning to Constantinople, immediately after the Young Turks' Revolution of 1908, he founded "La Ligue de l'initiative privée et de la decentralisation", his basic political platform being the internal autonomy of the Provinces while remaining united under the protection of the Ottoman flag and the Ottoman army in matters affecting the general policy and security of the Empire. But the chauvinistic policy of the Young Turks led them to dissolve Sabah-al-Din's Decentralization League in November 1908.[35] Later, sometime in 1912, a number of leading men of thought and experience among the Syrian, Lebanese and Palestinian *émigrés* in Cairo, formed a political party, with the knowledge of the Turkish Government, which they called the *Hizb al-Lamarkaziyah al-Idariyah al-'Uthmani*. This political party was public and open to any Ottoman, Arab or non-Arab who sympathized and supported its aims and its program.[36]

This party published a statement describing the advantages of decentralization in a multi-national, multi-racial Empire such as the Ottoman and gave for the purpose of its founding, the safe-guarding of the Empire from external pressure and internal conflicts and the rallying of its peoples round the focal centre of the Empire's unity, "the Ottoman Throne". This explanatory preamble was followed by the Program of the Party containing sixteen articles, the following four of which convey a clear idea of its aim:

Article 1. — "The Ottoman State *(Dawlat)* is a Constitutional State with a representative parliamentary Government. Every one of its *vilayets* is an inseparable part of the Sultanate which is itself indivisible under all circumstances. But the local administration of every *vilayet* will be on the basis of decentralization, it being understood that the Sultan will appoint the *Wali* and the Chief Judge.

Article IV. — In the capital of every *vilayet*, there will be organized a "General Assembly", an "Administrative Council", a Council on Education and a Council on *Awqaf*.

Article XIV. — Every *vilayet* will have two official languages. Turkish and the "local" language of its inhabitants.

Article XV. — Education in every *vilayet* will be in the language of the inhabitants of that *vilayet*.[37]

The *Fatat* and the Decentralization Party of Cairo held an Arab Congress in Paris from June 18 to 23, 1913 in the Hall of the Geographic Society at the Boulevard St. Germain.

The speeches delivered by the delegates and the deliberations during the six days of its sittings all emphasized the need of reforms on the basis of decentralization.[38] There was no discussion on and no demand for *separation* from the Ottoman Empire.[39] Indeed, Iskandar 'Ammun, the Vice-President of the Party, summed up the aims and the political purpose of Decentralization in the following words when he delivered his address:

"The Arab *Umma* (nation) does not want to separate itself from the Ottoman Empire...All that it desires is to replace the present form of government by one more compatible with the needs of all the divers elements which compose that Empire, in such wise that the inhabitants of any Province *(vilayet)* will have the final word in the internal administration of their own affairs.[40]

"We desire an *Ottoman* Government, neither Turkish nor Arab, a Government in which all the Ottomans have equal rights and equal obligations so that no party or group may deprive any other party or group from any of its rights or usurp them, for reasons of either race or religion, be it Arab, Turk, Armenian, Kurd, Muslim, Christian, Jew or Druze.[41]

After the coming of the Young Turks to power, Arab grievances were directed against the despotism and excessive centralization of the Government at Constantinople. Their rejoicing following the proclamation of the Constitution had ended in great disappointment. They believed that the Ottoman Empire being composed of divers races and nationalities with their different tongues, habits and traditions, could not be ruled effectively under that system of Government. They wanted a constitutional and representative Government which was truly constitutional and truly representative of the nation. Their Government was only in name constitutional and representative. The different elements which composed the Empire did not have equal rights and equal opportunities. The Governing body was restricted primarily to one element: The Turkish. This element was in a commanding and privileged position. Moreover, it pursued the policy of dissolving in its own Turkish matrix the Arab element. As a result of this policy, the Committee of Union and Progress insisted that Turkish should be the official and the only language of the Empire. This "Turkification" process became another great cause of Arab dissatisfaction with the Young Turks.

Sir Edwin Pears wrote that the Committee "would have no language but Turkish"—and wished to make of their heterogeneous subjects "a nation which should be one in language". The study of Turkish became compulsory in every school. Orders were given to change the name of the streets into Turkish, although "it may fairly be said that in most cities in Turkey not one-twentieth part of the population can read Turkish."[42] Dr. 'Abd- al-Rahman Shahbandar has related two experiences which he had in 1910.[43] First, Kamil Bey al-Solh told Dr. Shahbandar. "When I was on my way from Monastir to Damascus to take charge of the Court of Cassation, I converged on Constantinople at the request of the Minister of Justice Najm-al-Din Munla Bey. The latter warned me that the language of my Court had to be henceforth Turkish, because he said: 'we shall abandon the Arabs'." Secondly, "When we were in the Central Committee of Union and Progress in Syria," wrote Dr. Shahbandar, "we received oral instructions from the Central Office of the Committee through Dr. Muharram Bey asking us to make Turkish the language of all our communications with the said Committee." There was thus a deliberate attempt, adds Dr. Shahbandar to make the Turkish language supersede the Arabic in Arab lands.

The policy of substituting the Turkish for the Arabic language was doomed to failure right from the beginning. It was impossible to impose the Turkish language upon the Arabs. Indeed, the Turkish language itself had, probably by cultural and religious necessity, become greatly enriched by both the Persian and the Arabic languages. But it must be remembered that Arabic was the language in which the Qur'an had been revealed. The Muslims believe that as a medium of communication between Him and His people, in the days of the Prophet, God chose the Arabic language in its purest from which was the dialect of the tribe of Quraysh to which the Prophet Muhammad himself belonged. Consequently, the Muslims consider the language of the Qur'an sacred and therefore as eternal and unchangeable as their Holy Book itself. The following passages from the Qur'an emphasize the fact that God's revelation to the Prophet was made specifically in Arabic: "An Arabic Qur'an have we sent it down, that ye might understand it".[44] "Verily, from the Lord of the Worlds hath this Book come down...In the clear Arabic tongue".[45] "Had we made it a Qur'an in a foreign tongue, they had surely said, 'Unless its signs be made clear...' What! in a foreign tongue and the people Arabian?"[46] No one who is not acquainted with the cascading beauty of the Arabic language of the Qur'an, now mighty and thunderous in expression, now gentle and soothing in its poetical charm, can begin to comprehend its almost hypnotic effect on Arab Muslims throughout the world. Indeed, the Muslims consider the language of the Qur'an a great miracle of Islam. They believe in the i'jaz of the Qur'an, i.e. in the impossibility of imitating it, for it is "the most perfect example of style and language."[47]

The Turks, as Muslims, had a great veneration for the Arabic language and had Arabicized the Turkish language to an extraordinary extent. But as a conquering race, they were conscious of being the "Master race" and the master nation among the mosaic of races and nationalities which they governed. The Young Turks would not sacrifice their nationality and their race for the benefit of Islam, particularly at a time when the number of Arabs in the Ottoman Empire was probably greater than that of the Turks. They were more anxious than ever to keep the Empire Turkish and to preserve their privileged and dominating position; hence the attempt, though evidently too late in the day, of Turkifying the non-Turkish elements by first trying to impose upon them the Turkish language.[48] Consequently, all Arab reformers and Arab secret societies included in their program the necessity of having the Arabic language as the official language of the Arab provinces of the Ottoman Empire.[49]

In 1912 and 1913, the two Balkan Wars ended disastrously for the Young Turks. Almost all of European Turkey was lost. Whatever doubts the Committee still had as to which policy should be the basis of the building up of a new Turkey, were settled by those Wars, for "the shock of this disaster penetrated to wider circles than had been affected by the academic movement of the previous years, and seems to have kindled a genuine desire for national regeneration among all educated Turks."[50]

The anti-Arab and anti-Muslim spirit of this new Turkish nationalism expressed itself openly and violently during the two years immediately preceding the World War. Of the many societies which were formed with Government inspiration and support, in order to promote Pan-Turanianism, the most famous was the "Turk Ojagi" ("The Turkish Hearth") with its headquarters in Constantinople and many branches in the towns and villages of Anatolia. The Pan-Turanian ideas penetrated deep into the Turkish army and created very unpleasant feelings between the Arab and Turkish officers.[51]

The Arabs, meanwhile, continued to press for reforms and to assert their demands.[52] The Beirut Committee of Reform, com-

posed of eighty-six members from all the *"Millet* Councils" representing every religious denomination in that town held its first
meeting on January 12, 1913. At its third meeting, on January
31, the assembled delegates drew up a program of reforms composed of fifteen articles. In its preamble, the Ottoman Government was defined as "a constitutional representative Government."
The first article said that the external affairs of the *Vilayet* of
Syria, the army, customs, post and telegraph, legislation and taxes
were to be in the hands of the central administration, while the
internal affairs were to be placed under a General Council of the
Vilayet. (This Council would have the authority to depose the
Vali by a two-thirds majority vote). The fourteenth article stated
that the Arabic language was to be recognized as the official
language of the *Vilayet* and as an official language, like Turkish,
in the Chamber of Deputies and the Senate.[53] The answer of the
Turkish authorities was to dissolve the Beirut Reform Committee,
arrest its leaders and close its "club".[54] If the population wanted
any reforms, they were told to ask the Parliament to enact them.[55]

Meanwhile, the Western world was beginning to become
conscious of a new question: the Arab Question. In 1914, Ludovic
de Contenson wrote: "...Il y'a une question syrienne ou plutôt
dans un sens plus vaste, une question arabe. Chez les peuples,
dorénavant, la conscience nationale s'éveille avec une effrayante
intensité, au fur et à mesure que la littérature, la presse, les sou-
venirs nationaux, le sentiment de la valeur et même de la supériorité intellectuelle du conquis sur le conquérant affirment ou
avivent un nouvel état de choses. Et, parallèlement, dans l'âme
populaire percent des idées plus nettes de droit, de justice, d'éga-
lité, de l'organisation des sociétés musulmanes, fondées sur l'iné-
galité sociale, sur la supériorité du musulman sur le giaour."[56] The
author adds: "En Syrie, ce qui donne une particulière gravité à la
situation, c'est que la population musulmane a pris la tête du mouvement. 'Il y a depuis quelque temps', écrivait M. Debbas dans
l'Opinion du 15 février dernier, 'quelque chose de changé en Turque d'Asie. Les musulmans de Syrie, jusqu'ici réfractaires à l'idée
séparatiste, commencent à s'y rallier plus ou moins ouvertement...'

"D'ailleurs, depuis que l'Europe a reconnu aux Albanais,

musulmans et chrétiens, le droit de se gouverner eux-mêmes en tant que nationalité, sans que les Turcs conservent le droit de s'immiscer dans leur administration, on aurait mauvaise grâce à refuser aux Syriens ce que les Albanais ont eux-mêmes obtenus.

"La logique est du côté Syrien, si l'on s'en tient aux principes posés par la politique européenne. Nous ne blâmons pas l'Europe d'avoir ainsi reconnu le principe des nationalités, même musulmanes, dans l'Empire Ottoman. Mais nous sommes convaincu que ces principes de décentralisation sont destinés à prendre de l'extension et à porter de nouvelles conséquences dans l'avenir. Ce qu'il importe, c'est de concilier la politique de décentralisation, au point de vue syrien, avec le respect de l'intégrité ottomane en Turquie d'Asie."[57]

As we approach the eve of the World War, a word must be said about the tentative Franco-British understanding about "Syria". Raymond Poincaré writes in his *Memoirs* that in 1912 there were rumours of a British move in Syria "where most of the inhabitants looked to France for protection". But on December 5 of that year, Sir Edward Grey told the French Ambassador, Paul Cambon: "We have no intention of doing anything whatever in Syria, where we have neither aspirations nor designs"; a phrase, adds Poincaré, which "the Secretary of State willingly allowed me to quote to Parliament". "But it is needless to tell the Senate", continues Poincaré, quoting his own address to the Senate, "that in Lebanon and in Syria we have special and long-seated interests which we must see respected. The British Government in the most friendly manner has declared that in that part of the world it has no political aspirations and no wish or intention to do anything."[58]

On January 13, 1913, Sir Edward Grey wrote to Sir R. Rodd, the British ambassador in Rome about his conversation with the Italian ambassador in London: "I said that we ourselves had no designs in Asia Minor. All that we desired was the maintenance of a satisfactory "status-quo" which would secure the Persian Gulf and its littoral against disturbance. But Russia had special interests in Asia Minor owing to her strategic frontier; Germany had vested interests in the Anatolian and Baghdad Railways; and France had the Syrian Railways. I thought that all or any one of them might raise objections to a self-denying ordinance as to Asia Minor."[59]

But the German documents contain a different story. Prince Lichnowsky, the German Ambassador in London from 1912-1914, wrote: "When I came to London in November 1912, ... Sir Edward Grey...had not given up the idea of reaching an agreement with us...With Herr von Kuhlmann, the capable and business—like Envoy, as intermediary, an exchange of views was in progress concerning a renewal of the Portuguese Colonial Agreement and concerning Mesopotamia (The Baghdad Railway), the unavowed object of which was to divide the colonies in question, as well as Asia Minor, into spheres of interest."[60]

However, the entry of Turkey into the World War on the side of Germany found Britain and France still without a definite plan for the partition of the Near East into "spheres of influence" and "independent Arab areas". Hence, all the unhappy complications and conflicting promises which followed during and immediately after the War, in order, first, to define then to reconcile Anglo-French interests and finally to satisfy Arab national aspirations.

NOTES
AND REFERENCES

1. Heyd, Uriel, *Foundations of Turkish Nationalism*, p. 130.
    The American Ambassador, Henry Morgenthau, says of the
Young Turks that they "were not a government; they were really
an irresponsible party, a kind of secret society, which, by intrigue,
intimidation and assassination, had obtained most of the offices of
state." For an elaboration of his views on the Young Turks, see
Morgenthau, Henry, *Ambassador Morgenthau's Story*, (New York,
1918) pp. 11-19.

2. Les Jeunes-Turcs ne sûrent même pas gagner la confiance des A-
rabes qui constituaient l'élément musulman le plus nombreux de l'Empire. Pendant toute cette période, les tribus de la Syrie et de la Méso-
potamie étaient en effervescence continuelle, et le mouvement auto-
nomiste grandissait parmi la jeunesse intellectuelle arabe.."—Mandelstam, A., *Le Sort de l'Empire Ottoman*, p. 30.

3. "It was at Aleppo that I made acquaintance with the Turkey which
had come into being on July 24, 1908. Even among those whose
sympathies were deeply engaged on behalf of the new order, there
were not many Europeans who, in January 1909, had any clue to
public opinion outside Constantinople and Salonica. The events of
the six stirring months that had just elapsed had yet to be heard and
apprehended, and no sooner had I landed in Beyrout than I began
to shed European formulas and to look for the Asiatic value of the
great catchwords of revolution. In Aleppo, sitting at the feet of many
masters, who ranged down all the social grades from the high official
to the humblest labourer for hire, I learnt something of the hopes
and fears, the satisfaction, the bewilderment, and the indifference of
Asia. The populace had shared in the outburst of enthusiasm which
had greeted the granting of the constitution—a moment of unbridled
expectation when in the brief transport of universal benevolence, it
seemed as if the age-long problems of the Turkish empire had been
solved with a stroke of the pen; they had journeyed back from that
Utopia to find that human nature remained much as it had been
before. The public mind was unhinged; men were obsessed with a
sense of change, perplexed because change was slow to come, and
alarmed lest it should spring upon them unawares. The relaxation of
the rule of fear had worked in certain directions with immediate
effect, but not invariably to increase of security. True, there was a
definite gain of personal liberty. The spies had disappeared from
official quarters, and with them the exiles, who had been condemned
by 'Abdu'l Hamid, on known or unknown pretexts, to languish help-
lessly in the provincial capitals. Everywhere a daily press had sprung
into existence and foreign books and papers passed unhindered
through the post. The childish and exasperating restrictions with which
the Sultan had fettered his Christian subjects had fallen away. The
Armenians were no longer tied to the post whereon they dwelt; they
could, and did, travel where they pleased. The namusiyeh, the identi-

fication certificate, had received the annual government stamp without delay, and without need of bribes. In every company, Christian and Moslem, tongues were unloosed in outspoken criticism of official dealings, but it was extremely rare to find in these freely vented opinions anything of a constructive nature. The government was still, to the bulk of the population, a higher power, disconnected from those upon whom it exercised its will. You might complain of its lack of understanding just as you cursed the hailstorm that destroyed your crops, but you were in no way answerable for it, nor would you attempt to control or advise it, any more than you would offer advice to the hail cloud. Many a time have I searched for some trace of the Anglo-Saxon acceptance of a common responsibility in the problems that beset the State, a sense the germs of which exist in the Turkish village community and in the tribal system of the Arab and the Kurd; it never went beyond an embryonic application to small local matters, and the answers I received resembled, mutatis mutandis, that of Fattuh when I questioned him as to the part he had played in the recent general election. "Your Excellency knows that I am a carriage-driver, what have I to do with government? But I can tell you that the new government is no better than the old. Look now at Aleppo; have we a juster law? wallah, no!"—Bell, Gertrude Lothian, *Amurath to Amurath*, pp. 3-5.

4. *Handbooks No. 96c & d.*, pp. 21-22.

5. Gooch and Temperley, vol. IX, Part I (No. 38) Confidential, enclosure in F.O. 371/1014, pp. 208-209.

6. Great Britain, F.O. 371/1014 (No. 635) Confidential. *Ibid.*, p. 207.

7. Knight, p. 64.

8. *Handbooks, No. 96a & b.*, p. 68.

9. *Ibid.*, pp. 65-66.

10. *Handbooks No. 96a & b.*, p. 68, citing *Mechroutiette* (Paris, December 1913) p. 58.

11. *Ibid.*, pp. 68-69.

12. France, Paris, Bibliothèque Nationale, under Library index No.$\dfrac{8\ 0^3g}{779}$

13. *Handbooks No. 96a & b.*, p. 67.

14. *Handbooks No. 96c & d.*, p. 18.

15. Seton-Watson, *The Rise of Nationality in the Balkans*, (London, 1917) pp. 135-136.
    Seton-Watson adds: "The real brains of the movement were Jewish or Judaco-Moslem. Their financial aid came from the wealthy Dunmehs and Jews of Salonica, and from the capitalists—international or semi-international— of Vienna, Budapest, Berlin and perhaps also of Paris and London..."—*Ibid.*, pp. 134-135.

"The Jews of Salonika, generally known as *Dunmés* (converts) were the real parents of the Turkish revolution. They are a definite people—Hebrews, but indefinable as to creed. The popular verdict was that they were only nominal Moslems and were true followers of the Pentateuch...At that time, only the most industrious student of the Near East knew of their existence. There was no man to prophesy that the *Dunmés* were to be the chief authors of a revolution whose results were to shake the world."—Herbert, Aubrey, *Ben Kendim,* pp. 15-16.

16. It is believed that the idea was taken from the book of a French savant, M. Léon Cahun—*Introduction à l'Histoire de l'Asie : Turcs et Mongols, des origines à 1405,* in which M. Cahun's theme was that the "Turanians" were originally a brilliant race which later degenerated when they abandoned the law of the steppes and adopted Muslim culture. Dr. Nazim, a prominent member of the Committee of Union and Progress, is said to have been converted to Pan-Turanianism by a copy of this book which was lent to him by the French Consul-General at Salonika.—See *Handbooks No. 96c & d.,* p. 23, n. 1. See also Emin, Ahmed, pp. 187-199.

17. "A pseudonym which is believed to cover the name of Albert Cohen, a Salonika Jew." See *Handbooks No. 96 c and d.,* p. 18.

18. In addition to many articles in the Turkish press, Akçuraoglu, Yusuf, published *Uç Tarzi Siyaset* (Cairo, 1903 ; Istanbul, A.H. 1327).

19. Consult Heyd. See also Hostler, Charles W., *Turkism and the Soviets* (London 1957) pp. 115-146.

20. For extracts from *Qawm Jadid,* see *Al-Manar,* vol. XVII, Part 7, June 1914, pp. 539-544.

21. Toynbee and Kirkwood, *Turkey,* p. 57.
    Toynbee and Kirkwood add: "The practical bearing of this propaganda lay in the fact that two-thirds of the Turkish-speaking peoples of the world were to be found within the frontiers, not of Turkey but of Russia, so that Pan-Turanianism offered a lever for breaking up the Russian Empire." p. 57.

22. *Handbooks, No. 96c & d.,* pp. 45-47.
    For an account in Arabic and Turkish of the anti-Arab and anti-Muslim policy of the Committee of Union and Progress, see *Thawrat al-'Arab* (anonymous) pp. 138-161.

23. See *Al-Hilal,* vol. XVII, Part 7, April 1909, p. 415.

24. Broadly speaking, the Arab tribes of Arabia have been divided into two main divisions: the northern and the southern. The northern tribes are called 'Adnanites and the southern ones Yamanites. According to Arab genealogists, Qahtan was the ancestor of all Yamanites.

25. For a detailed account of these societies, their founders, their purpose and their activities, see Sa'id, A. *Al-Thawrat al-'Arabiya al-Kubra* (Cairo, n.d.), vol. I, pp. 6-50 and Antonius, pp. 107-121.

26. Antonius, p. 111.

27. *Ibid.,* p. 109.

28. George Antonius has reported *(Arab Awakening,* p. 111, n. 2) that Tawfiq al-Natur was "hanged by the Turks during the war..." The truth is that he was condemned to be hanged by the Turkish military court in 'Aley. But while in prison, he was shot and severly wounded by one of the guards. When the time for his hanging came, he was still in the military hospital in Beirut. Consequently, he was exiled, for the rest of the war, to a remote village in Anatolia. The author is indebted to Tawfiq al-Natur himself for most valuable information on the *Fatat* society.

29. Literally, "the Society of those who use the letter *Dâd*". *Dâd* is the fifteenth letter of the Arabic alphabet. The Arabs claim that this letter is found only in their alphabet and that its correct pronunciation is the test of a true Arab.

30. See *Al-'Azm,* pp. 136-144.

31. Edib, Halidé, *Conflict of East and West in Turkey,* (Lahore, India, 1935) p. 98.

32. Heyd, p. 131.

33. See also *Al-Manar,* vol. XVI, Part 7 (July 4, 1913). p. 547.

34. See *Al-Hilal,* vol. XVII, pp. 17-26. Consult also Tunaya, pp. 315-344.

35. Mandelstam, pp. 14-16.

36. Its President was Rafiq Bey al-'Azm, a member of a well known Muslim family in Damascus. He died in 1925. For the history, Constitution and program of the Party see *al-Manar,* vols. XVI and XVII, 1913-1914, articles by Muhammad Rashid Rida and others; also Sa'id, vol. I, pp. 14-18, and Antonius, pp. 109-110.

37. See *Al-Manar,* vol. XVI, Part 3 (March 8, 1913) pp. 229-231.

38. "The list of delegates bore the names of twenty-five accredited persons of whom twenty-four attended. The membership was almost exactly divided between Moslems and Christians and the delegates were preponderantly Syrian. Iraq was represented by two members and three others came on behalf of Arab communities in the United States."—Antonius, p. 115.

39. For the Resolutions passed at the Congress, see Appendix C.

40. See Khairallah, K.T. *Les Régions Arabes Libérées,* pp. 48-52, citing article in *Le Temps* of June 10, 1913, based on an interview with 'Abdu'l Hamid Zahrawi, and also pp. 52-54 citing an account of the decisions reached at the Arab Congress, written by Charles Debbas (one of the secretaries of the Congress) and published in *La Correspondance d'Orient* of July 1, 1913.

41. *Al-Mu'tamar al-'Arabi al-Awwal,* pp. 103-104.

42. Pears, Sir Edwin, *Forty Years in Constantinople,* p. 271.

43. See the Memoirs of Dr. A. Shahbandar, published under the title of *Al-Thawrat-al-Wataniyah* (Damascus, 1933) pp. 2-3.

44. Sura 12, "Joseph, Peace Be on Him", v. 2 (Rodwell's translation).

45. Sura 26, "The Poets", v. 194.

46. Sura 41, "The Made Plain", v. 43.

47. The Prophet himself had challenged not only men, but even the "spirits"—the *"Djinn"*—to produce anything like it: "Say, verily, were men and *Djinn* assembled to produce the like of Qur'an, they could not produce its like, though the one should help the other."—Sura 17, The Night Journey, v. 90.

48. It was in vain that a few years earlier, Jamal-al-Din al-Afghani had recommended to Sultan 'Abdu'l Hamid, just the opposite process of substituting the Arabic language—"the language of that pure religion" (i.e. Islam)—as Sultan Selim had once proposed, for the Turkish. In so doing, he told the Sultan, Turkey as a Muslim Power and the Sultan as the Caliph of Islam would acquire far greater prestige and power in the Arab and Muslim world. Jamal-al-Din thought the Turks were committing a grievous error by trying to Turkify the Arabs.—Al-Makhzumi, M., *Khatirat Jamal-al-Din al-Afghani al-Husaini,* pp. 236-237.

49. See *Al-Hilal,* vol. XVIII, Part 3, December 1, 1909, pp. 161-163, and *Al-Muqtabas,* vol. IV, Part 2, (Damascus, 1909) pp. 109-112.

50. *Handbooks No. 96 c and d.,* p. 19. It should be remembered that after the coup d'état of January 26, 1913 when Nazim Pasha, the Minister of War was shot dead and Kamil Pasha, the Grand Vizier, was forced to resign, the Young Turks obtained supreme power over the destiny of Turkey.

51. After the publication of the book *Qawm Jadid* (A New Nation) a very strongly worded article expressing anti-Arab sentiments and anti-Arab criticism appeared in the well-known Turkish newspaper *Eqdam.* It caused a furore among the Arab youth, mainly students, who were living in Constantinople. They organized a demonstration and marched to the editorial office of *Eqdam* which they attacked with stones breaking the glass of its windows. Then a delegation of them went to the Prime Minister and protested against the publication of that humiliating article.

     The article had also great repercussions in the Arab Provinces of Turkey. Syrian and Iraqi newspapers rose in defense of the Arabs and were bitterly indignant against the Turks.—See Al-A'zami, *Al-Qadiyah al-'Arabiyah,* pp. 102-109. See also Tunaya, pp. 375-386.

52. "Au mois de décembre, 1912, le gouverneur de Beyrouth, télégraphiait à son gouvernement : "Le pays est travaillé par différentes influences.

Pour améliorer sa situation devenue intolérable, une partie de la population se tourne déjà, ou vers l'Angleterre ou vers la France. Si nous ne prenons l'initiative des réformes, le pays nous échappe".—Khairallah, p. 39.

53. See *Al-Manar*, vol. XVI, Part 4, April 7, 1913, pp. 275-280.
54. The agitation was such in Beirut against the Governor's arbitrary action that he was obliged to release the leaders. In this connection, the Beirut Correspondent of the French paper *Temps* wrote to his paper on March 18: "... Chekri Asly bey, ex-député de Damas au Parlement et promoteur du mouvement réformiste dans cet important centre, est appelé à Beyrouth où le Gouverneur lui propose un poste de sous-gouverneur à Lattaquié: — Ce ne sont pas des postes lucratifs, lui répond Asly bey, que nous, *Arabes*, nous réclamons, ce sont des réformes sérieuses, garanties dans leur application par les puissances de l'Empire...

"Et c'est actuellement cette même parole que repètent tous les Syriens ainsi que les populations de rives de l'Euphrates et des bords de la mer Rouge.."—Khairallah, p. 40.
55. "Telle est la réponse du grand vizir Said Pacha au télégramme des 1,300 notables Beyrouthains, adréssée au vali de Beyrouth:

'Nous avons reçu un télégramme de Beyrouth signé de plusieurs personnes, demandant l'autorisation pour le comité de réformes de se réunir de nouveau. Si les habitants veulent des réformes, ils doivent les demander au Parlement ; et si, la majorité du Parlement les accepte, le Gouvernement les exécutera. Comme les habitants veulent fonder ds comités et faire des demandes contraires à la loi, le Gouvernement ne peut pas prendre ces demandes en considération...' "—Aboussouan, Benoît, *Le Problème politique Syrien*, p. 61.

Sharif 'Ali Haidar who was highly respected by the Turks and was loyal to them, and who at the same time understood and sympathized with the Arab grievances, tried to reconcile the two parties. He brought together Talaat Bey, the leader of the Young Turks and 'Abd-al-Karim al-Khalil, the Chairman of *Al-Muntada al-Adabi* with the hope that they will agree on some reforms favourable to the Arabs. Actually, an agreement on an eleven-point program of reforms was reached and signed by Talaat Bey and 'Abd-al-Karim al-Khalil. But shortly after, it was unfortunately denounced and rejected by the Young Turks' Government.—For the Turkish and Arabic texts of that Agreement, see *Al-Manar*, vol. XVI, Part 8 of August 2, 1913, pp. 638-639. See also Djemal Pasha, *Memories of a Turkish Statesman, 1913-1919*, pp. 58-59.
56. Contenson, Avant-Propos p. 3.
57. *Ibid.*, p. 68.
58. *The Memoirs of Raymond Poincaré*, translated and adapted by Sir George Arthur, (London 1926) vol. 1, pp. 336 and 338. The French text of these Memoirs is entitled: *Au Service de la France*. 10 vols. (Paris, 1926...32).
59. Gooch and Temperley, vol. IX, *The Balkan Wars*, p. 404.
60. *The Times Documentary History of the War*, (London, 1919) vol. IX, part 3, pp. 3-4.

CHAPTER VI

THE EMERGENCE OF ARAB NATIONALISM

Part 2 — The War Years, 1914 - 1918

On October 30, 1914, the British Ambassador at Constantinople demanded his passport and the next day, at 5.05 p.m. G.M.T. the following fateful message was sent out by wireless from London—"Admiralty to All Ships": "Commence hostilities at once against Turkey. Acknowledge."[1] In the seven words of that cable lay the final collapse of the Ottoman Empire and the beginning of unforseen events and incalculable forces which gave birth to the present Arab states in the Near East.

We have seen how for many years, the British Government helped to maintain the integrity of the Ottoman rule in Asiatic Turkey which, of course, included the Arab lands. On the eve of the First World War, Britain still refused to join with the other Powers in partitioning the Turkish possessions in Asia. On June 27, 1913, Sir Edward Grey wrote to Sir E. Goschen, British Ambassador in Berlin: "Respecting Asiatic Turkey, I had observed that there were two possible courses. One was to consolidate the remaining Turkish dominions and to put Turkey on her feet... The other course was a division of Asiatic Turkey into spheres of interest. This would lead to partition and to the complete disappearance of the Turkish Empire." The German Ambassador, this despatch continues, told Sir Edward Grey that "the Arabs seemed to be rather restless, and an Arab Chief from Nejd had already made advances to the Germans, apparently on the assumption that Turkish rule was being broken up; but the Germans had declined to entertain his advances..." And Sir Edward Grey replied that "we also had had advances of the same sort made to us from Chiefs, I thought more in the region of Busra (sic!) and the

Persian Gulf; but we had not encouraged them because they pre-supposed a break up of Turkish authority. Amongst other things, it would give great offence to Moslem opinion in British terri-tory if we took part in a policy of destroying the Turkish Govern-ment and dividing its territory."[2] In a telegram to Sir G. Buchanan, British Ambassador in Constantinople dated July 4, 1913 (one year before the War) Sir Edward Grey wrote: "A grave question of policy is involved and *the only policy to which we can become a party is one directed to avoid collapse and partition of Asiatic Turkey.* The effect of the opposite course upon our own Mus-sulmans in India would be disastrous to say nothing of the com-plications that would be produced between European Powers."[3]

However, no sooner had hostilities begun on November 5 than the British Press made it clear what fate awaited Turkey. On November 3, *The Times* wrote: "Turkey has betrayed the interests of Islam by making wanton war on the Allies, and has thereby pronounced her own death sentence". Among other papers which predicted the same fate for Turkey was the *Daily Mail* which wrote on November 23: "That the Ottoman Empire in Europe, won by the sword, is now about to perish by the sword we have no doubt whatever", and the *Daily News* of November 31 which said: "If Germany is defeated the punishment of Turkey for partnership with Germany will be practical annihilation as a Power."

No evidence has come to light yet to show whether the British Cabinet itself had any clear plan for her own share of the spoils in the Near East. Nearly five months after the opening of hostilities, Sir Edward Grey told the French Ambassador, M. Cambon: "The Cabinet here had not yet had time to consider our desiderata"[4] (concerning the Turkish possessions in Asia)... The Cabinet, however, seems to have reached one conclusion: "I said that we had already stipulated that, when Turkey disappear-ed from Constantinople and the Straits, there must, in the inter-ests of Islam, be an independent Moslem political unit somewhere else. Its centre would naturally be the Moslem Holy Places and it would include Arabia. *But we must settle what else should be included.* We, ourselves, had not yet come to a definite opinion whether Mesopotamia should be included in this independent

Moslem state, *or whether we should put forward a claim for ourselves in that region."*[5]

The India Office, on the other hand, was very definite about the necessity of bringing Mesopotamia directly or indirectly under British rule for the protection of India and British security in the Persian Gulf. Writing a Minute, on September 26, 1914, on "The rôle of India in a Turkish War," Sir Edmund Barron, military secretary of the India Office was strongly in favour of an expedition being sent to occupy Basra, and he concluded his Minute in the following words:

"This seems the psychological moment to take action. So unexpected a stroke at this moment would have a startling effect:

(1)   It would checkmate Turkish intrigues and demonstrate our ability to strike.

(2)   It would encourage the Arabs to rally to us, and confirm the Sheikhs of Muhammara and Koweit in their allegiance.

(3)   It would safeguard Egypt, and without Arab support a Turkish invasion is impossible.

(4)   It would effectually protect the oil-installation at Abadan. Such results seem to justify fully the proposed action."[6]

When Turkey joined the Central Powers in 1914, British policy towards the Asiatic provinces of the Ottoman Empire was determined by the fact that these provinces occupied an area which was of tremendous strategic importance to the prosecution of the War.

As these provinces were inhabited mainly by Arabs and as these Arabs had already shown various degrees of dissatisfaction towards Ottoman rule, it was natural and logical that the British should "attack the Turkish Empire through its Arab subjects".[7] Hence all the efforts made by the British and all the promises and pledges given by them to the Arabs to win them to their side. "As a feature of the general strategy of the war", wrote Lloyd George, "the elimination of Turkey from the ranks of our enemies would have given us that access to Russia and Roumania which was so disastrously lacking, and without which they were driven out of the war...The course of the war would have been altered and shortened...The Turkish Empire lay across the track by land or water to our great possessions in the East...It was vital for our communications, as it was essential for our prestige in the East, that once the Turks declared war against us, we should defeat and discredit them without loss of time. The importance of a speedy victory over the Turks for the security of the British Empire was undeniable.."[8] Hence, the British turned towards the "disaffected population" of the Turkish Empire—the Arabs. The ground had already been prepared and the soil was fertile.

When the Ottoman Empire entered the World War on November 5, she sealed her own doom. The Sick Man, at last, committed suicide.[9]

In that hour of destiny the Empire was ruled by a triumvirate of three brave and ruthless men: Enver, Talaat and Djemal. They were ably supported by "the skillful and incorruptible Finance Minister, Djavid".[10] These Turkish leaders were apparently convinced that Germany would win the war on land.[11] Tewfik Pasha, the Turkish Ambassador in London, told Sir Wyndham Deedes: "We firmly believe that if the Entente wins, Turkey will be divided up—Syria to France, Armenia to Russia, Persian Gulf hinterland to England. On the other hand, Germany will probably, if her group win, leave us what we have. Our obvious duty is to throw what weight we can into the scale against the Allies and with Germany".[12] Every effort made by Britain, France and even Russia to keep Turkey out of the war had proved in vain; especially as the Turks saw in the Anglo-Russian Convention of 1907 "a definite alliance between the Power who had been Turkey's strongest and most disinterested supporter and friend with the Power who was her ancient and inexorable enemy."[13] "Nothing could supplant in the Turkish mind the fear of Russia...the sense of peril from the North still outweighed all else in Turkish thoughts."[14]

Meanwhile, the Arabs found their lands plunged in a war they had not wanted. A small minority secretly rejoiced that the collapse of the Ottoman Empire was imminent and thus "the hour of retribution and restoration was at hand." It is true that the vast majority of the Arabs remained loyal supporters of the Caliphate and the Sultanate, but some of the Arab leaders found it imperative for the Arabs to leave the sinking Ottoman ship and establish their independence even if it were necessary to seek "foreign" help. Nor was this "foreign" help lacking. Both France and Britain had been waiting for this moment. They were aware of the grievances of the Arabs against the Turks and particularly of the dissatisfactions of Sharif Husain, Emir of Mecca. Nearly seven months before the war, Britain had actually been approached for help but at that time the help had naturally been declined as she could "never entertain the idea of supplying arms to be used against a Friendly Power". The approach had come from Emir 'Abdullah, second son of Sharif Husain both to Lord Kitchener and to Ronald Storrs to whom he had "unlocked his heart during his visit to Cairo".[15] Now, however, the situation had radically changed. Hence, the following two historic cables from Lord Kitchener, Secretary of State for War, cables which were the official starting point of the British invitation to the Arabs to revolt:[16]

"Sept. 24, 1914. To H.M.'s Representative in Cairo. Following from Lord Kitchener. Tell Storrs to send secret and carefully chosen messenger from me to Sharif Abdallah to ascertain whether 'should present armed German influence in Constantinople coerce Sultan against his will, and Sublime Porte, he and his father and Arabs of the Hejaz would be with us or against us.' "[17]

On October 31, Lord Kitchener cabled again:

"Salaams to Sharif Abdallah. Germany has now bought the Turkish Government with gold, notwithstanding that England, France and Russia guaranteed integrity of Ottoman Empire if Turkey remained neutral in the War. Turkish Government have against will of Sultan committed acts of aggression by invading the frontiers of Egypt with bands of Turkish soldiers. If Arab nation assists England in this war England will guarantee that no intervention takes place in Arabia and will give Arabs every assistance against external foreign aggression."[18]

It is not the purpose of this chapter to describe or discuss the protracted negotiations which followed. However, some of their salient points may be worth repeating here. Upon receipt of the above cable, Storrs sent a letter to Emir 'Abdullah with a secret messenger. The latter returned with "a long and favourable reply" from 'Abdullah. On December 10, the same messenger returned from a second visit to Sharif Husain who "was friendly but unable to break with the Turks immediately". "The first definite proposals from the Sharif reached Sir Henry McMahon[19] in July, 1915 (with a personal letter from Abdallah to myself, unsigned and undated) when he solicited the support of His Majesty's Government for the cause of Arab independence, and proposed certain boundaries for the independent Arab area."[20]

We must now turn to the events in Syria. Djemal Pasha says in his *Memories of a Turkish Statesman* that about ten days after Turkey's entry into the war, Enver Pasha, the Minister of War invited him to his house and told him, among other things, that "the news from Syria points to general disturbance in the country and great activity on the part of the revolutionary Arabs. In these circumstances, I have wondered whether Your Excellency would not give a further proof of your patriotism by taking over the command of the 4th Army."[21] The result of this interview was that Djemal Pasha arrived in Syria in December 1914 as Commander-in-Chief of the IVth Army "to start an offensive against the Suez Canal to keep the English tied up in Egypt...and also to maintain peace and internal order in Syria."[22] He tried at first to win the Arabs by what he called "a policy of clemency and tolerance."[23] In a speech which he delivered in Damascus early in January 1915, he said: "Gentlemen, the programme for the welfare of the Arabs which our party means to carry out in its entirety is more comprehensive than anything you can imagine. I myself am not one of those who think it a harmful or dangerous thing that the two races, Arab and Turkish, should secure their unity while remaining separate nations, subject to the same Khalif... Today, I am in a position to assure you that the Turkish and Arab ideals do not conflict. They are brothers in their national strivings, and perhaps their efforts are complementary..."[24] He also emphasized that the war was essentially a *Jihad* in defence of Islam and a great Muslim Power—the Ottoman Empire.

Although it is very difficult to pass a fair and balanced judgment on any man who has been placed in authority, under abnormal and highly critical circumstances, there is much evidence to warrant the statement that Djemal Pasha seems to have been, essentially, a very ambitious and despotic man. Soon after his arrival in Syria he instituted a reign of terror, through executions and deportations. After the failure of his Expedition against the Suez Canal in February 1915, he returned to Syria and carried out a ruthless policy towards many Arab leaders by condemning them to death as "traitors" who wanted, through Decentralization, to dismember the Ottoman Empire and "sell their countries to the foreigner". On August 21, 1915, eleven Arab notables (ten Muslims and one Christian) were hanged at *al-Burj,* the principal square of Beirut and on May 6, 1916 another batch of twenty-one most prominent Muslim and Christian leaders (seventeen Muslims and four Christians) were executed at dawn; fourteen went to the gallows in Beirut and seven in *al-Marjeh* square in Damascus.

There were also from time to time other executions of single individuals both in Syria and Lebanon. No less than seventy-one other notables were condemned to death in absentia. Many families were exiled to remote regions in Anatolia and much property was confiscated. The following American document of May 1916 is of much interest: "Turkish authorities appear to be pursuing policy of Turkifying Syria and adjacent Arabic-speaking provinces. Many notables both Christian and Moslem are stated to have been arrested imprisoned and executed...I understand that Turks put forward as ostensible reason for this action that Syrians and other Arabs subjected to this treatment were disloyal to the Turkish Government, that they held meetings in Egypt and elsewhere to consider and decide steps to be taken for the separation of Syria from the Ottoman Empire..."[25]

Moreover, because of the blockade of the Allies and the fact that Djemal Pasha was collecting the produce of the country for the Turkish and German armies, and also because of the greed of certain wheat merchants and their callous disregard of human suffering, thousands among the inhabitants became paupers and many thousands perished from starvation and disease. To make the scarcity of food worse, clouds of locusts descended on Syria, Lebanon, and Palestine ravaging the crops. Djemal Pasha took up his own defence in his *Memories* and in the *Red Book* which was published in Constantinople in 1916[26] containing photostatic documents of correspondence between some of the Arab leaders

and the French Government[27], with which he tried to show that
those leaders were traitors to Turkey by being in secret communication with the enemy, particularly with France and that
Syria was on the verge of rebellion against the Turkish rule. It
must be remembered, of course, that at the time of the execution
of the Arab leaders, the British attack on the Dardanelles had
already begun and British troops had landed at Gallipoli. A large
number of Arab and Turkish troops had been despatched from
Syria to the scene of those decisive battles on which hung the fate
of Turkey and Russia. Djemal Pasha was naturally worried lest the
Allies should make landings on the coast of Lebanon and be
helped by fifth-columnists in the country—people who, he knew
for certain, had been in communication with Foreign Powers.

But many of the documents in the *Red Book* when read
carefully do not justify his wholesale accusations against the Arab
leaders and some of his statements in his *Memories* are untrue.
A number of these documents are contradictory and others clearly
demonstrate that their authors did not want separation from the
Ottoman Empire, although they worked for local independence.
Might it not be that one of Djemal Pasha's real motives for these
condemnations was the fear of losing his own life should his own
"secret negotiations with the enemy" become known in Constantinople, as a result of the indiscretions of one of the Arab leaders,[28]
to whom he had confided his secret designs? There seems to be
little doubt that he was in communication with Russia and with
France with the intention of getting out of the war on condition
that he would be allowed to build up for himself an independent
state from the Arab provinces of the Ottoman Empire.[29] The secret
documents in the Russian Tzarist archives throw much light on
this matter.[30]

However, whatever the motives were, the consequences of
Djemal Pasha's anti-Arab policy were to widen still further
the gulf between Arabs and Turks and thus to intensify the Arab
struggle to obtain their independence. Indeed, it may not be an
exaggeration to say that Djemal Pasha's rule in Syria was one of
the determining factors which helped most of the Muslim Arab
leaders to make up their minds once for all to break away completely from the Turkish Empire.[31] After the executions of May

6, 1916, Arab nationalism gathered momentum and strength. Arab political independence and Arab national sovereignty became a tangible reality and an absolute necessity for sheer survival if for no other reason.

If Djemal Pasha's oppressive rule in Syria was the second decisive factor[32] in the consolidation of Arab nationalism, the third equally decisive factor was the Allied encouragement and support of the Arabs to rebel against the Turks and gain their freedom and independence. Lloyd George wrote in his *War Memoirs:* "Our agents among them (the Arabs), who included men long skilled in the arts of Oriental diplomacy, encouraged this attitude of rebellion, and promised them arms and ammunition..."[33] It is significant that the *Jihad* or Holy War which was proclaimed by Turkey against the Allies at the beginning of the War failed to produce any effect in the Arab provinces. Liman von Sanders remarks in his memoirs that this Holy War bore an appearance of unreality because Turkey was allied with Christian States, and German and Austrian officers and men were serving in the Turkish army.[34] Speaking of this *Jihad,* Halide Edib says: "But such was the irony of fate that not only were there Moslems fighting in the French, English, and even Russian armies, but Turkey's own Moslem subjects, chiefly Arabs, were in league with the enemy camp."[35]

We have already noted how Kitchener got in touch with Sharif 'Abdullah through Storrs and how, as a result, an exchange of letters took place between Sharif Husain and Sir Henry McMahon. The final outcome of these negotiations was the Arab Revolt which started in Mecca on June 10, 1916, under the leadership of Sharif Husain,[36] and with the military and financial support of Great Britain.[37] The story of this revolt is not our concern here. It has been related in a literary masterpiece: T. E. Lawrence's *Seven Pillars of Wisdom,* in the Introduction of which Lawrence wrote:

"Some Englishmen of whom Kitchener was chief, believed that a rebellion of Arabs against Turks would enable England, while fighting Germany, simultaneously to defeat her ally Turkey. Their knowledge of the nature and power and country of the Arabic-speaking peoples made them think that the issue of such a rebellion would be happy: and indicated its character and method. So they allowed it to begin, having obtained formal assurances of help for it from the British government. Yet none the less the rebellion of the Sherif of Mecca came to most as a surprise, and found the Allies unready. It aroused mixed feelings and made strong friends and enemies, amid whose clashing jealousies its affairs began to miscarry."[38]

It must be recorded in all historical fairness that by no means all the Arabs and Arab leaders in the Arab provinces of the Ottoman Empire were in favor of being ruled by Sharif Husain of Mecca. Nor were they all united as to their understanding of Arab independence or the ultimate form of Government in Arab lands. The following is an excellent summary of the conflicting Arab interests as recorded by Sir Wyndham Deedes who was in the Egyptian branch of the British Intelligence Service and of whom it has been said that he had "the most exhaustive knowledge...of the play and counter-play of forces in the Turkish Empire..." Under the date of February 21-29, 1916, Deedes writes: "But into the network of conflicting interests was woven an even more tangled thread: the Arab question. In addition to the Turkish parties we have some three Arab parties here:

"(1)   Those representing the Syrians, who are mainly concerned with the future of Syria, and their general concern in the matter is that the French should not be allowed to go to Syria, that they should have no more at the very outside than economic and financial concessions. So great is their dislike of the French that it is very questionable that if the French were to reign today in Syria they would not drive the Moslems straight away into the hands of the Turks...It is difficult rather to account for this extraordinary dislike and, if asked, they quote Tunis and other places where the French have colonies of Moslems. The Christians too are by no means yearning for the French, in fact, with the exception of the Maronites, the Christians of Syria are as opposed to the French going there, by which I mean territorial concessions, as are the Moslems. How difficult this makes our position at the present moment is quite obvious, because we ourselves know that our F. O. have made some sort of arrangement with the French by which we believe they are to have some territorial aggrandisement....News of this is only (now) reaching our friends who are continually coming to us and asking whether it is true we have sold them to the French.

"(2)   We have the party of the Shereef. With this party we really are negotiating on the lines of a spiritual and temporal Arab Kingdom. That at all events is what the Shereef wants. Personally, and I think it is the view of most of us, and is the view of many of the Arabs and all of the Turks themselves, this idea is not a practical one. For...it will never be possible to get all the Arabs of Syria, Iraq, Yemen and the others to acknowledge one temporal chief, even if they acknowledge one spiritual chief. And if they were prepared to acknowledge one man the question is who that man is to be. The Shereef of Mecca's influence is accepted over a certain part of the countries named but not over others...The Shereef's (party) is much the most moderate and sensible of all...they are very loyal to us for their own ends; secrecy being vital they are very anxious that none other than their own party should have wind of what is going on...

"(3)   Finally, we have the party of Iraq. They want an independent Government for those parts and they are very anxious to get out of us now what zone we mean to allot and, if they can, what form of Government. Now our *great difficulty* is the Indian Government, who view all our flirtations with these parties with the greatest suspicion and particularly any arrangements made about Iraq, Basra and the Persian Gulf.

"What with the French and the Indian Governments our difficulties sometimes appear insuperable. It should be noted, too, that the Turkish parties, especially those that incline most to the present form of government, or who are anxious to see some form of government of the Rahmi-Prince Sabahattin type set up again in Turkey, view this Arab movement with the greatest misgiving..."[39]

Meanwhile, the three Great Powers, Great Britain, France and Russia, were defining "their own respective claims in Turkey-in-Asia". "The resulting secret agreement between the three Powers about the disposal of Asiatic Turkey, known as the Sykes-Picot Agreement, was signed in May 1916, and its terms were afterwards published by the Bolsheviks when the Petrograd archives fell into their hands."[40]

For an understanding of what the future had in store for the Arab Near East, as far as Britain was concerned, it is of great interest to be acquainted with the following two significant documents both of which were written in 1917. The first is a British "Statement on Foreign Policy made to the Imperial War Council". It was communicated to the American Secretary of State, Mr. Lansing, in Washington on May 18, 1917, by Mr. Balfour, Chief of the British Special Mission which was then visiting the United States. The policy concerning Turkey was as follows:

"The practical destruction of the Turkish Empire is undoubtedly one of the objects which we desire to attain. The Turks may well be left—I hope they will be left—in a more or less independent position in Asia Minor. If we are successful, unquestionably Turkey will be deprived of all that in the larger sense may be called Arabia; she will be deprived of the most important portions of the Valley of the Euphrates and the Tigris; she will lose Constantinople; and Syria, Armenia and the southern parts of Asia Minor will, if not annexed by the Entente Powers, probably fall more or less under their domination."[41]

The second document discusses "The Asiatic Provinces of Turkey" and reads, in part:

"If I were to set myself to make a brief for the Turk I should not be without arguments. No one who knows him and his history can cause him of having been the sole agent of destruction in the lands he governed. A heavy burden of blame lies upon the nations of Europe, for whom Turkey has been a pawn in an age-long and shameful game of jealous cupidity. But the time for such pleas is past. It has been blotted out by the blood and tears of the subject races. Venit summa dies et ineluctabile tempus—let us consider what the new day should bring.

"I take it for granted that the Arab provinces cannot be allowed to remain under Turkish rule...We are dealing with one of the most important agricultural areas in the world. The Iraq alone is not second in productiveness to Egypt, while in acreage, it is more than twice as large; the Syrian granaries, without modern facilities to transport, helped to feed Rome, and the commerce of the ancient as well as of the medieval world flowed of

necessity to eastern industrial centres...The rehabilitation of the
Near East may once more alter the balance, or let us say establish
a just balance, by recreating a market which has been for centuries
in abeyance. It will add immeasurably to the wealth of a universe
wasted by war and provide new fields for the reviving industries
of Europe...East and West will once more be linked together by
common advantage."[42]

The story of the Arab rebellion, the rôles of Lawrence and
Faisal in carrying out the "Revolt in the Desert" and triumphantly
terminating it in Damascus on October 1, 1918, the Anglo-French
promises of "independence" to the Arabs, on the one hand, and
on the other, the secret negotiations and treaties among the Allies
themselves concerning their own spheres of direct and indirect
rule in Arab lands based on their own interpretation of the word
"independence", have been the subject of bitter controversy during the last three decades.[43] They do not fall within the scope of
this essay for they do not belong to the history of Arab-Turkish
relations but are part of a broader and more complicated phase
in the history of the relations between the East and the West in
Arab lands.

The last year of the war saw the final collapse of the Ottoman Empire and the occupation of the Near East by the Allied
armies. Early in January 1918, British forces (The Egyptian Expe-
ditionary Force) invaded southern Palestine and on December 9
occupied Jerusalem. Nine months later, in one big onrushing wave,
Allenby's army swept through the rest of Syria and Lebanon
defeating the Turkish IVth army. Haifa was accupied on September 23, 1918, Damascus on October 1 and Beirut on the 8th.
By one of those striking ironies of fate, the final surrender of
the Turkish army came on the very plain of Marj Dabiq where
almost exactly four hundred years earlier, the troops of Sultan
Selim had won a decisive victory—the victory which made the
Ottomans masters of this very Syria which they had now lost to
the Allies. Aleppo was captured on October 25 and the next day,
the last engagement of the war against Turkey in the East, took
place some eight miles north-west of the city. Five days later,
came the news of the armistice.[44] The armistice with Turkey was
not, however, signed on land but on board a British battleship,

the *Agamemnon* in the harbour of Mudros at Lemnos, in the Aegean Sea, on October 30.[45] The 25th and last article of the Armistice read: "Hostilities between the Allies and Turkey shall cease from noon, local time, on Thursday, 31st. October 1918."[46] Article 16 stipulated "the surrender of all garrisons in Hejaz, Assir, Yemen, Syria and Mesopotamia to the nearest Allied Commander."[47]

With the signing of the Armistice, Arab-Turkish relations as they had existed for four hundred years came to an end. The subsequent developments in Arab lands belong to a new phase in the history of the Arab Near East.

NOTES
AND REFERENCES

1. Churchill, Winston, S., *The World Crisis, 1911-1918* (London, 1939), vol. I, p. 495.

2. Gooch, and Temperley, vol. X, Part I, pp. 465-466.

3. *Ibid.,* p. 481. The italics are the author's.

4. Grey, E. *Twenty-Five Years,* vol. II p. 236: Dispatch of Sir Edward Grey to Sir F. Bertie, dated "Foreign Office, March 23, 1915".

5. *Ibid.,* The italics are the author's.

6. See Great Britain, *Mesopotamia Commission*—appointed under an "Act of Parliament" in August 1916, (London, H.M.S.O., 1917) p. 12.

7. Temperley, H.W.V., *A History of the Peace Conference of Paris,* vol. VI, p. 178.

8. Lloyd George, D., *War Memoirs.* (London, 1933-36) vol. IV, pp. 1802-1803.

9. It is interesting to note that before the opening of hostilities, Sharif Husain of Mecca wrote a personal letter to Sultan Muhammad Rashad, pleading with him not to enter the war on the side of Germany against Russia, Britain and France.—Ibn-al-Husain, (King 'Abdullah.) *Mudhakkarati,* pp. 98-99.

10. Actually, a Turkish Parliament was, theoretically at least, ruling the country. It was the third Parliament after the restoration of the Constitution in 1908 and was elected on the eve of the World War. It held its first session on May 14, 1914 in the presence of the Sultan. Out of a total of 245 members in that Parliament, only 69 were Arabs while 142 were Turks, the rest being Armenians, Greeks and Jews; also 209 were Muslims and 36 Christians.—*Al-Hilal,* vol. 22, Part 9 of June 1, 1914, p. 708.

11. When the Young Turks came to power, they tried to abrogate the Capitulations but the pressure of the Foreign Powers and the Balkan Wars prevented them from doing so. However, when the World War began, the Porte informed the Ambassadors of the Powers on September 9, 1914, of her decision to abolish the Capitulations beginning October 1st. The Powers refused to accept that decision but the abrogation went into force on that date. The Capitulations were officially abolished by article 28 of the Treaty of Lausanne, on July 24, 1923.

12. Presland, John, *Deedes Bey, A Study of Sir Wyndham Deedes, 1883-1923* (London, 1942), pp. 139-140.

13. Churchill, vol. I, p. 435.

14. *Ibid.*, pp. 433-434.

Talaat Pasha to Aubrey Herbert: "Rightly or wrongly, you made friends with Russia: that was your policy at home and that was your policy at the Embassy in Constantinople...If the leaders liked you (when we made our revolution) the people adored you ; they took the horses out of your Ambassador's carriage and they pulled it up to the Embassy...We Young Turks practically offered Turkey to you, and you refused us." Herbert, Aubrey, pp. 310 and 312-313.

15. "In April 1914 occurred a visit to Cairo the ultimate impact of which upon the War and the destinies of the Near and Middle East is not event yet fully calculable. The Amir Abdallah, second son of Husain, Grand Sharif of Mecca, arrived from Constantinople as the guest of the Khedive and was received by Lord Kitchener...Meanwhile, we were advised from Constantinople that such audiences were displeasing to the Sublime Porte, always suspicious of Arab intrigue in the Hejaz and in Syria...Travelling by a series of delicately inclined planes...I found myself...being categorically asked whether Great Britain would present the Grand Sharif with a dozen, or half a dozen machine guns...'for defense'...against attack from the Turks. I needed no special instructions to inform him that we could never entertain the idea of supplying arms to be used against a Friendly Power. Abdallah can have expected no other reply, and we parted on the best of terms."—Storrs, R., *Orientations*, pp. 122-123. Storrs quotes a private letter from Lord Kitchener to Sir W. Tyrrell dated British Agency, Cairo, April 26, 1914 which contains the following excerpt:

"Sharif Abdallah...He sent for Storrs who under my instructions told him the Arabs of the Hejaz could expect no encouragement from us and that our only interest in Arabia was the safety and comfort of Indian pilgrims..."

16. Wavell says: "The idea of binding the Arabs of the Hejaz to the British cause was suggested by Sir John Maxwell, as early as October, 1914." Major General Sir John Maxwell was in command of the British forces in Egypt in September 1914. See Wavell, A. P. *The Palestine Campaigns* (London 1928), note on p. 52.

17. Storrs, p. 149.

18. *Ibid.*, p. 152. It may be of interest to note that Kitchener's invitation to the Arabs of Hejaz to "assist England in this war" was not the only one of its kind. Lawrence writes, " 'Aziz el Masri, Enver's rival, who was living, much indebted to Egypt, was an idol of the Arab officers. He was approached by Lord Kitchener in the first days of the war, with the hope of winning the Turkish Mesopotamian forces on our side."—Lawrence, T. E., *Seven Pillars of Wisdom*, p. 59.

Moreover, the Mesopotamian leader Talib al-Naqib himself, as early as 1911, and a group of Arab deputies had appealed to Sharif Husain to "shake the yoke which weighed on the Arabs and to deliver them from tyranny and slavery".—Khairallah, pp. 32-33.

The appeal was repeated in 1915. "In January 1915, Yasin, head of the Mesopotamian officers, Ali Riza, head of the Damascus officers, and 'Abd-el Ghani el Areisi, for the Syrian civilians, sent down to him (Sharif Husain) a concrete proposal for a military mutiny in Syria against the Turks. The oppressed people of Mesopotamia and Syria, the Committees of the Ahad and the Fetah, were calling out to him as the Father of the Arabs, the Moslem of Moslems, their greatest prince, their oldest notable, to save them from the sinister designs of Talaat and Jemal".—Lawrence, p. 50.

19. Sir Henry McMahon was appointed in December 1914 as High Commissioner for Egypt. "He is slight, fair, very young for 52, quiet, friendly, agreeable, considerate and cautious."—Storrs, p. 191.

20. *Ibid.,* p. 152.

   The exchange of letters which took place between the Sharif and McMahon from July 14, 1915 to January 30, 1916, belongs to a complicated phase of secret negotiations and secret promises in which the Allies indulged, under the strain and stress of war, for the purpose of winning that war. The story of this Correspondence has already appeared in numerous publications. See Lawrence, chapters IV, V and VI; Antonius, pp. 164-183 and Appendix A. pp. 413-427; Storrs, chapter VIII *Cmd. 5957* (Miscellaneous No. 3: *Correspondence between Sir Henry McMahon, His Majesty's High Commissioner at Cairo and the Sherif Hussein of Mecca, July 1915—March 1916* (London, 1939), and *Cmd 5974: Report of a Committee set up to Consider Certain Correspondence between Sir Henry McMahon (His Majesty's High Commissioner in Egypt) and the Sherif of Mecca in 1915 and 1916* (London, 1939). See also Howard, H.N., *The Partition of Turkey,* pp. 187-193.
   For these and other negotiations with Ibn Sa'ud and the Shaikh of Kuwait and in general for the relations of Great Britain and the Arab peoples during the war, see Temperly, vol. VI, pp. 118-133.

21. Djemal Pasha, pp. 137-138.

22. *Ibid.,* "...Djemal himself, just before his train started made this public declaration: 'I shall not return to Constantinople until I have conquered Egypt' ".—Morgenthau, p. 171.

23. Djemal Pasha, p. 201.

24. *Ibid.,* pp. 199-201.

25. U.S.A., Department of State, Telegram (1821) from the Chargé d'Affaires in Turkey (Philip) to the Secretary of State (Lansing). See *Papers Relating to the Foreign Relations of the United States,* Supplement—The World War, 1914-1918 (Washington, 1928-1933) 1916 Supplement, p. 851.

26. *La Vérité Sur la Question Syrienne* (Stamboul, 1916); also published simultaneously in Turkish and Arabic.

27. "On the day of my arrival in Damascus, Hulussi Bey, the Governor-

General of Syria, told me he wanted to confer with me on extremely important matters. We met the same night at Government House. He handed me some very important documents which had been seized at the French Consulate, and told me that most of the documents implicated the most highly-placed and influential Mussulmans of Damascus, Beirut and other cities...

"Judging by these documents, there was not the slightest doubt that the Arab revolutionaries were working under French protection and, indeed, under the guidance and for the benefit of the French Government."—Djemal Pasha, p. 197.

Télégramme secret du Ministre à Berne.

No. 338   2/15 juin 1916

Je me réfère à mon 329

Mandelstamm demande de transmettre : "A propos des évènements de Syrie. J'apprends complémentairement que Djémal Pacha a adressé à la population de Syrie une proclamation dans laquelle il accuse les puissances de l'Entente de viser au partage entre elles, de l'Empire turc et explique l'exécution des Syriens par la découverte d'un complot fomenté encore avant la guerre et ayant pour but l'annexion de la Syrie à la France. Les Turcs auraient soidisant saisi au consulat français de Damas une correspondance établissant les rapports secrets des Syriens avec la France. S'il en est ainsi, ces papiers se trouvaient entre les mains du gouvernement turc depuis le début de la guerre et cependant ce dernier n'avait pas fait usage jusqu'à présent. C'est pourquoi on peut supposer qu'au cours des derniers temps de nouveaux évènements se sont produits qui ont décidé les Turcs à prononcer l'ostracisme contre les Syriens. En tout cas, les exécutions et les bannissments in-interrompus de Syriens vont provoquer fatalement de l'agitation dans tout le monde musulman et augmenteront la haine contre les Jeunes Turcs. Un fait également digne de remarquer est que le rôle principal dans ces persécutions est joué par Djemal Pacha qui a apparemment abandonné toute idée de rapprochement avec les puissances de l'Entente."—Marchand, René (ed.), *Un Livre Noir, Diplomatie d'avant-guerre et de guerre d'après les documents des archives Russes (1910-1917),* Tome Troisième, Livre III, Avril à Septembre, 1916, (Paris 1922-34) p. 67. See Djemal Pasha's Statement published in the newspapers of Syria on May 7, 1916—cited in *Thawrat-al-'Arab*, pp. 164-167.

28. It is reported that 'Abd-al-Karim al-Khalil who was the first to be executed, while standing at the foot of the gallows said: "I know the real reason for which Djemal Pasha is hanging me and it will be known to history one day." Sa'id, vol. I, p. 85.

29. "The Turkish world seemed to be disintegrating in Djemal's time, just as the Roman Republic was dissolving in the days of Antony; Djemal believed that he might become the heir of one or more of its provinces and possibly establish a dynasty. He expected that the military expedition on which he was now starting would make him not only the conqueror of Turkey's fairest province, but also one

of the powerful figures of the world."—Morgenthau, p. 172.

30. These negotiations are of such great interest to the history of the period and might have had such an incalculable effect on the course of the war and on the destiny of the Arab countries that it may not be out of place to give here a brief summary of them. The first document is dated October 26, 1915. It is a letter from Sazanoff to Russian Embassies in Paris and Rome referring to news he had received from "American circles" in Istanbul expressing Djemal Pasha's desire to undertake "a hostile act" towards the Porte—if his conditions were granted...—Djemal Pasha's primary condition was that he—and after him his children and grandchildren—should become "The Sultan of an independent federated state composed of Syria, Palestine, Iraq, Arabia, Cilicia, Armenia and Kurdistan"—under the guarantee of the Allies. In December 1915, news of this nature kept coming to St. Petersburg and later to Paris from Russian representatives abroad. But France was not sympathetic with Djemal's project because while it satisfied Russia by giving her Constantinople and the Straits, it deprived the French of fulfilling their ambition of having Syria, Palestine and a part of Cilicia. In another document dated January 17, Edward Grey is mentioned by Sazanoff, as believing that the French should directly negotiate with Djemal Pasha. On January 27, 1916, Britain made the Russian Ambassador, Benkendorff, understand that she was not interested to take part in the negotiations with Djemal. She was dealing directly with the Arabs for what was both to her and to the Arab's satisfaction. She was relying first and foremost on the Arabs alone, taking advantage of the hostile feelings towards the Turks and towards Djemal who had hanged their leaders. The last published communication in the Russian Archives, dated March 13, 1916, indicates the failure of the negotiations because of Anglo-French opposition...—See Sa'id, vol. I, pp. 168-175, and Polonsky, J., *Documents Diplomatiques Secrets Russes, 1914-1917* (Paris, 1928) Section VI, pp. 249-331 and particularly document No. 1999 of December 30, 1915. See also Pingaud, A., *Histoire Diplomatique de la* cember 30, 1915. See also Pingaud, A., *Histoire Diplomatique de la France pendant la Grande Guerre* (Paris, 1938-40) vol. III, pp. 142-143 and 228.

31. General Liman von Sanders, in a report to General Ludendorff, dated Constantinople, October 25, 1916, wrote: "En Syrie, les mesures de rigueur exagérées prises par Djémal Pacha ont détourné les Arabes de la cause turque. A Damas ont en lieu ce mois-ci des troubles assez graves, qui ont necessité l'intervention de la force armée." And speaking of Faisal, Liman von Sanders, adds: "La déplorable politique arabe du gouvernement turc en avait fait un adversaire acharné".—Sanders, Liman von, *Cinq Ans de Turquie* (Paris, 1923) pp. 166 and 240. "The effect of Ahmed Djemal Pasha's 'reign of terror' was not only to deprive Syria of almost all possible leaders of revolt, but to increase in the people the spirit of revolt. It crowned seven years of Ottomanising efforts by making Ottomanism impossible for Arabs."—Handbook No. 88, *Turkey in Asia*, p. 16.

32. The first, being the Chauvinistic policy of the Young Turks discussed in Chapter V above.

33. Lloyd George, vol. IV, p. 1810.

34. Sanders, Liman von, pp. 44-45.

35. Edib, Halidé, *Turkey Faces West*, (New Haven, 1930) p. 141.

36. Ibn-al-Husain (King 'Abdullah), pp. 108-152. See also Sa'id, vol. I, pp. 145-165.

For the full text of Sharif Husain's proclamation of June 26 addressed to "All his Muslim Brethren", see *ibid.*, pp. 149-157. It is significant that after giving the reasons for the revolt, the Sharif states its purpose to be "complete separation and independence" of "the Arab countries" from the Government of the C.U.P. and its goal: "the defence of the Muslim religion and the raising of the station of Muslims..." based on the foundation of the Shari'a Law, "the sole source of guidance and support."

37. Ronald Storrs states that the total cost of the Arab Revolt to the British taxpayer was £11.000.000. He writes: "In addition to the initial sum I took, Husain received from August 8th, 1916 £125.000 a month: in all, less than one million sterling. The remaining ten million represent military operations and supplies from Great Britain."—Storrs, p. 153, n. 2.

It should be added that the French Government, too, contributed its help which, though limited, nevertheless, in the words of Sir Reginald Wingate "assisted largely in the success of the joint operations in which they took a very gallant and conspicuous part." A French Military Mission, headed by Lieutenant-Colonel Brémond and composed of notable Muslim representatives of Algeria, Tunisia, Morocco, and French West Africa, arrived at Jeddah on September 20, 1916, bringing with it for Sharif Husain a subsidy of 1,250,000 gold francs. It was followed shortly by a small contingent of French forces and a small number of French machine guns—field artillery and rifles. The Mission was warmly welcomed by Sharif Husain. See Brémond, *Le Hedjaz dans la Guerre Mondiale* (Paris, 1903) pp. 48-53, 64-67, and 348,349.

38. Lawrence, p. 28.

39. Persland, pp. 244-245.

40. Toynbee, Arnold, J., *The Western Question in Greece and Turkey*, (London, 1922) p. 48. Toynbee adds in explanation the following footnote: "The final text of the agreement was drafted by Sir Mark Sykes and M. Georges Picot on behalf of the British and French Governments respectively, but these gentlemen only settled details of phraseology. The fundamental points in the agreement had already been worked out in conferences of leading statesmen and officials on both sides, before it was handed over to them for completion. The unofficial name, used for brevity, gives a wrong impression of the part they played, and now that the agreement is discredited and Sir

Mark Sykes unable to defend himself, owing to his lamentable death from influenza during the Peace Conference at Paris, it is important that no injustice should be done to his memory. The responsibility on the British side for this agreement lies with the British Government." For an official and authoritative account of the Sykes-Picot Agreement, see Woodword, E.L. and Butler, Rohan, *Documents on British Foreign Policy, 1919-1939*, First Series, vol. IV, 1919 (London, 1952) pp. 241-251.

41. U.S.A., Department of State, *Papers Relating to the Foreign Relations of the United States: The Lansing Papers, 1914-1920* (Washington, 1940) vol. II, p. 23.

42. *Iraq—Memo, No. 20* dated July 25, 1917 and written by "the Chief Political Officer in charge Iraq Section, Arab Bureau, Baghdad" to "the Officer in Charge, Arab Bureau, c/o Director, Military Intelligence, Cairo".

This Memo was addressed to:

1) Secretary of State for Foreign Affairs, London, S.W.
2) Foreign Secretary to the Government of India in the Foreign and Political Department, Simla.
3) Political Secretary, India Office, London, S. W.
4) Chief of the General Staff, I.E.F. "D", G.H.Q.
5) Secretary to the Government of India, Army Department, Simla.

43. The issues being further complicated by the Balfour Declaration of November 2, 1917 concerning "the establishment of a Jewish national home in Palestine".

44. "In less than six weeks Allenby's army had captured 75,000 prisoners and 360 guns, and had moved its front forward 350 miles."—Wavell, Viscount, *Allenby, Soldier and Statesman*, (London, 1946), p. 245.

45. The four signatories were Vice-Admiral Sir S.A. Cough-Calthorpe, British Commander-in-Chief in the Mediterranean; Ra'uf Bey, Turkish Minister of Marine, Rashad Hikmat Bey, Under-Secretary for Foreign Affairs, Lieutenant Colonel Sa'dallah Bey, Turkish General Staff.—See Falls, Captain Cyrill, *History of the Great War, Military Operations, Egypt and Palestine*, from June 1917 to the End of the War, Part II (London 1930) p. 625.

46. *Ibid.*, p. 627.
47. *Ibid.*, p. 626.

CHAPTER VII

CONCLUSION AND POSTSCRIPT

The Arab Near East, bent under the weight of a long history and an old civilization, has been shaken out of its lethargy and thrown into a state of flux and confusion during the last four decades. The changes that have overtaken it have been bewilderingly rapid and, in some cases, profoundly disturbing because they have not been the result of slow and natural growth from the soil of its own history but have been thrust upon it, suddenly and forcibly from without. The time for adjusting to these changes and assimilating them has been exceedingly short. Hence one must be extremely cautious to draw any final "conclusions" from the kaleidoscope of events which have succeeded one another in these lands. In this concluding chapter, the author will try to sum up certain fundamental issues and problems in the background history of the Arabs under the Turks, which he has described in the previous chapters. In that background, four factors stand out: Islam, the Turks, the impact of the West and Arab nationalism.

If the Turkish rule lasted for four hundred years in Arab lands and if the Arabs acquiesced in that rule most of that time, it is essentially because the Turks were Muslims.

The Ottoman sultans as *Ghazis* continued the expansion of Islam, after its fortunes had reached their lowest ebb with the destruction of Baghdad in 1258 at the hand of Hulagu and his horde of Mongolian conquerors. The Turks invaded Europe, the heart of Christendom and carried the banner of Islam to the very gates of Vienna. Since the occupation of Spain by the Arabs and the battle of Poitiers in 732 A.D., the Christian nations had neither felt nor been shaken by the Power of a Muslim nation as they were for nearly three hundred years by the might of the Ottoman sultans. The Arabs as Muslims were proud of Turkish power and prestige. The Ottoman Empire was their Empire as much as it was the Turks'. These facts must be remembered and must be taken into consideration for any study of Arab-Turkish relations and for any understanding of the Arab attitude towards the West. But, unfortunately, many students of contemporary Arab history are either uninformed or, looking through the coloured glasses of modern political and secular nationalism, deliberately ignore and therefore fail to comprehend the religious background of the forces which for centuries influenced and moulded the Arab Near East —Islam.

Hence for a correct understanding and appraisal of the Arab Near East, today, a study of Islam, Muslim institutions and Muslim psychology is imperative. Lacking this basic inquiry, other studies will touch only the surface and not the heart of the matter. Those who see nothing in the Arab Near East but its geography and geopolitics, its overland commercial routes, its principal airfields, its strategic coastline and mountains, and its rich oil fields are making a grievous error. The forty-two million human beings in this area are today the most important element in the strategic value of this region to the Western Powers. Failure to understand this human element has been one of the major causes of the failure of the West in the Arab Near East. To understand fully these people one must understand the source from which spring their motives and actions, namely, the religion of Islam; without this it will be impossible to comprehend the deeper issues at stake. Many political, economic and social problems in this part of the world are interwoven with religion. The force of Islam is still much greater than the force of politico-secular nationalism. But, so far at least, the West seems to have either ignored or underestimated this basic truth.

It is also time for Western historians to abandon some of their long cherished misconceptions about Arab-Turkish relations. Taking the latter part of the nineteenth and the beginning of the twentieth centuries as their observable starting points, at a time when corruption in the Ottoman administration was reaching its nadir and Arab-Turkish relations were strained severely both because of the short-sightedness of the Turks themselves and because of the political machinations of the Western Powers, they have projected this picture into the previous 375 years of Turkish rule in Arab lands and have reached the conclusion that the Arabs "suffered" for four hundred years under the yoke of Turkish mis-government and despotism! Nothing is further from the truth than this assertion.

It is true that the Ottoman Empire was composed of a mosaic of races, nationalities and religions which the Turks did not attempt either to unite by force or to "Turkify". But it must be remembered that during the greatest part of Turkish rule the Arabs did not consider the Turkish rule as a "foreign" rule. The word "foreign" did not have in those days the twentieth century political connotation of a *nationally* alien and, often, politically "undesirable" person. The world in which the Arabs and the Turks lived together was in the nineteenth century sense of the term, *politically* a non-national world. The vast majority of the Arabs did not consider the Turks as "foreigners"—except when the Turkish leaders themselves, after 1908, ceased to be considered in Arab eyes as good Muslims and defenders of Islam and as brothers in the Faith.

It is thus unjustifiable to regard the Turks as the oppressors of the Arabs except in the last years of Turkish rule during which time the Turks suffered at least as much as the Arabs from Turkish misgovernment. Numerous facts and accounts support the conclusion that the Turkish government before its decline and fall was, on the whole, orderly and reasonable in the treatment of its subjects. For nearly three hundred years, the Ottoman administration in Arab lands compared favourably with that of most of the governments of Europe.

On the other hand, the Western world of the nineteenth century was going through a great transition as a result of powerful re-volutionary forces embodied in industrial capitalism, in the development of technology and in the growth of militant nationalism. There was also a process of secularization which was gaining momentum in the social and governmental institutions of the Western countries. Thus, at a time when the European nation-states were growing in military and economic power, in governmental organization and in scientific progress, the Ottoman Empire seemed to be standing still and stagnating. This brings us to the third factor: the impact of the West on Arab lands.

For many years, prior to the First World War, the Arab knowledge of the West was through the medium of trade and was limited by what the Arabs had read and heard about it. A few had a first hand knowledge of the West through their travels a-broad. Their attitude towards that West was, on the whole, one of respect for its military might, admiration for its material pro-gress and achievements and for its honesty in business transac-tions. The "word of an Englishman" was proverbial for its in-tegrity and reliability. A European—a *Franji*—was, in general considered as a civilized and superior being. "When I first heard the East a-calling to me, now, I regret to say, nearly fifty years ago", wrote Sir Valentine Chirol, "the enduring supremacy of the Occident over the Orient was almost universally assumed as a matter of course. The Western nations claimed it in virtue of their superior civilization and were able to enforce it by the superior material and economic equipment..."[1]

It is regrettable that when the Arabs came in actual contact with the West in their own lands, during and at the end of the First War, it was with a military and political West. It is true, of course, that the Arabs in Egypt and Palestine, had seen and heard the guns of Napoleon I from 1799 to 1801, but that was a short-lived occasion with short-lived results. In the twentieth century, however, the situation was vastly different. The great shock the Arabs had was their awakening to that kind of a West which by the very nature of the circumstances of the time, was primarily and inevitably coloured by the Machiavellian spirit of power—politics. At first, they were jubilant at the liberation of their coun-tries from the horrors of war. Later, they became disillusioned and disheartened at the failure of their national aspirations and the lack of success which accompanied the political experiments which were tried in their lands. New political systems and philo-sophies were imported into the Near East under the general term of democracy and grafted artificially onto a society which was feudal in nature and theocratic in spirit. The results were not happy, and were often disappointing. The strain and stress pro-duced by maladjustments and by the lack of understanding, and sometimes of appreciation, of the new political institutions, discredited democracy in the eyes of many Easterners. It is too often forgotten that democracy is not an article of export, and there is no automatic guarantee that, just because the outward symbols of democracy are created in an alien soil, democracy itself will suddenly prevail.

It is true, of course, that Westernization in its material technological aspects could not be stopped nor was it probably desirable to stop it. Indeed, there seemed nothing wrong in improving the physical conditions of life whether in building new roads, improving health conditions, constructing better houses, riding in cars, using telephones, enjoying the blessings of electricity and of better means of communication and transportation. But the cultural-spiritual heritage of the West was not wanted—except by a small group of "Westernized" Easterners. The Arab-Muslim reformers while admitting the necessity of improving and remodelling the internal conditions in Arab lands had no intention of introducing a Western pattern of culture nor did they believe in its superiority. To them and to the vast majority of the masses behind them, the return to the purity of Islam and Muslim institutions was the answer to all the evils which surrounded them. They were, indeed, opposed to "spiritual Westernization" and preached against it as "dangerous" and "heretical". For they saw in it a double danger to their lands and to their peoples: the political danger of Western imperialism encroaching upon the Arab provinces and the spiritual danger of either Western Christian culture imposing itself upon Islam or the Western materialistic philosophy of the Machine Age submerging the new and future generations of Arab youth in its agnosticism and in its secularism. The reaction and protest of the Arabs against the ascendency of the West, against its partition of the Near East into mandates and zones of influence, found expression more and more violently in the most potent of all the new forces generated recently in this part of the world, namely the force of Arab political nationalism. Neither the speed nor the scale of this force had been foreseen.

It has often been said that the Arabs experienced a national *awakening* as a result of the impact of the West on them in the nineteenth century. There is no satisfactory historical evidence for this contention. If by Arab awakening be meant the awakening of Arab *national consciousness,* then the term "awakening" is a misnomer. Throughout the four centuries of Turkish rule, the Arabs remained conscious of their religion, *Islam,* and of their language, *Arabic.* They never ceased to think of themselves as *Arabs.* Indeed, the vehemence with which the Arabs opposed the Turkifying policy of the Young Turks is in itself a proof that their Arab consciousness was wide awake. Had Arab consciousness been submerged and destroyed by the Turks as is commonly asserted, the Young Turks would have had very little difficulty in "Turkifying" the Arab lands. Nationalism has undergone several changes in meaning during the course of its evolution in various States. But if we take into consideration, basically, the racial, cultural and spiritual concept of nationality, we find that Arab nationalism is one of the oldest nationalisms in the world.

The true birth of Arab nationalism took place with the rise of Islam. Even as a generalization, there is no support for the contention that Arab nationalism was born as an "intellectual movement" in literary circles and secret societies and especially through the fiery poems of Arab poets. Islam was revealed by an Arabian Prophet, in the Arabic language, in Arabia. We read in the Qur'an: "A Messenger has now come to you from among yourselves..."[2] There is a tradition that the Prophet said one day: "I am an Arab, the Qur'an is in Arabic and the language of the denizens of Paradise is Arabic". And according to another tradition, he is reported to have stated: "He who loves the Arabs loves me, and he who hates them hates me." The Arabs could not help feeling that they were a "chosen race". It was the Muslim Arabs of Arabia that the Prophet glorified in these words: "Ye are the best people *(Umma* or "nation") that hath been raised up unto mankind."[3] One of the basic aims of Islam was to replace the narrow blood and tribal ties existing among the Arabs in pagan days or the "Days of Ignorance" by a broader, a wider "religious patriotism" found in Islam itself. The Arabs were to be united into one great community, the Community of the Faithful—the *Umma* or the "nation" of Islam. "Verily, you are the people of one 'nation' and I, your Lord; therefore, worship me."[4] The Arab nation was, thus, a nation originally born out of Islam. This "religious nationalism" remains an indelible part of the hearts and minds of the Arabs.

When Islam became the religion of such non-Arabs as the Persians and the Indians, the Arabs felt still more conscious of their Arabism, and continued to consider themselves supreme over the nations of their "clients". The Arab Muslims believed that they had "conferred" a great favour upon the "foreign" Muslims by "having rescued them from unbelief." During the Umayyad Caliphate (661-750 A.D.), Arab national consciousness and Arab prestige were, perhaps, at their peak. "The Arabs... believed themselves at this time to be superior to all other nations, whether clients or members of tolerated creeds. In his own opinion, the Arab was born to rule, and everyone else to serve; whence, at the commencement of Islam, the Arabs occupied themselves only with governing and politics; all other occupations, especially arts and crafts, were relinquished by them to non-Arabs. An Arab and a client had a dispute in the presence of 'Abdallah ibn 'Amir, governor of Iraq, when the client said to the Arab: 'God give us few like thee!' The Arab retorted: 'God give us many like thee!' Being asked why he blessed in answer to the other's curse, he replied: 'Do not these people sweep our streets, patch our shoes, and weave our garments?'"[5] As late as the middle of the nineteenth century, an "Oriental Student" observed that "Damascenes consider themselves, on the double ground of being Moslems and Arabs, as the noblest race in the world, and that the government of the Sultan is the first in rank, not because he is Malek-er-Roum, or sovereign of the Greek Empire, but the Caliph, or successor of Mohammed."[6]

Arab national consciousness survived throughout the centuries, in spite of all the vicissitudes of the Arabs during their long history, because two of the strongest ties of national unity, in the broad sense of the term, were never destroyed: the linguistic and the religious. The Arabs continued to *feel* as Arabs, because they continued to speak one language and believe in one religion. Their cultural and spiritual ties remained far stronger than either territorial unity or geographical separation. Hence the Arabs never lost or "forgot" their "nationalism" under the Turks, especially as the Turks made no attempt, except at the eleventh hour—to

"Turkify" the Arabs. All that the Arab leaders wanted at first—the masses were still indifferent—was that the Arab provinces *within the Ottoman Empire* should have an independent Arab government. They believed that the best form of government for the multi-national, multi-racial Ottoman Empire was a decentralized government. Some had in mind visions of an Ottoman "Commonwealth of Nations". As to *complete separation* from the Ottoman Empire, the idea was only in the minds of few extremists among the Muslims, before the Turkish Revolution of 1908. Its exponents and real supporters were primarily the Christians of Lebanon. But after 1908, the idea was almost forced upon some Muslim Arab leaders by the short-sightedness and chauvinistic Pan-Turanian policy of the Young Turks. The despotic policy of Djemal Pasha, Commander-in-chief of the IVth Army in Syria, during the first World War when he ordered the hanging of prominent Arabs in Beirut and Damascus, widened still further the breach between the Arabs and the Turks and greatly intensified the Arab leaders' desire to break away completely from the Ottoman Empire. Finally, the promises of the Allies, again during that War, to "liberate" the Arabs from the Turks and to give them their "independence" led to the Arab Revolt which started in Mecca on June 10, 1916, under the leadership of Sharif Husain.

Thus, if by Arab Awakening be meant the desire of the Arabs to separate themselves from the Turks and establish an independent, sovereign Arab State, similar to European states, this certainly was not so much an awakening, as the desire for self-determination and political independence. What the educated and enlightened Arabs were waking up to was not to Arab consciousness which had never "slept" but to an independent political life. This was part of the general political awakening which had occurred in Europe two hundred years earlier and more recently in Asia. The moving and motivating force was a demand by the Arabs for their political rights, for social justice, and for liberty. It was essentially man's eternal quest for freedom and justice. This "political nationalism" which marks the second stage in the development of Arab nationalism was primarily a product of political and social conditions prevailing during the last years of Turkish rule in Arab lands. But even then, religion was not

divorced from Arab nationalism. Not only the vast majority of
the Arabs were Muslims, but together with the goal of self-
determination and selft-government went the further aim of rising
to the defence of Islam, restoring its past glories and raising the
Arabs—"the race by means of which God had led the peoples
(of the world) from darkness to light"—to their rightful place
under the sun, the glorious place which God had destined for
them, as His own "chosen Umma".[7]

The first leaders of Arab political nationalism, particularly
Sharif Husain of Mecca, envisaged, immediately before and during the first World War, an Arab State rising out of the dissolution
of the Ottoman Empire, built around an Arab Muslim King
and on Muslim foundations. In a memorandum submitted to the
Peace Conference on January 1, 1919, Emir Faisal wrote: "The
country from a line Alexandretta—Persia, southward to the Indian
Ocean is inhabited by 'Arabs'— by which we mean people of
closely related Semitic stocks, all speaking the one language,
Arabic...

"The aim of the Arab nationalist movements (of which my
father became the leader in war after combined appeals from
the Syrian and Mesopotamian branches) is to unite the Arabs
eventually into one nation..."[8]

And again, in a second memorandum to the Peace Conference, on January 29, 1919, the Emir wrote: "As representing
my father, who, by request of Britain and France, led the Arab
rebellion against the Turks, I have come to ask that the Arabic-
speaking peoples of Asia, from the line Alexandretta-Diarbekr
southward to the Indian Ocean, be recognized as independent
sovereign peoples under the guarantee of the League of Nations..."[9]

The Sykes-Picot Agreement of May 16, 1916 was trans-
formed into a Mandates system by the Allied Supreme Council
meeting at San-Remo, from April 19 to 25, 1920, as a result
of which, Iraq and Syria were recognized as "two independent countries" under the tutelage of Great Britain and France
as Mandatory Powers, "until such time when they would be able
to stand alone." The presence of the Mandatory Powers intensified the struggle for self-determination and political independence,
gave birth to a number of political parties and consolidated op-

position to the West. This post-war period may be considered as
the third stage in the evolution of Arab nationalism. It is a period
of frustration and disappointment in the Western promises of
independence which the Arab leaders had, unfortunately, inter-
preted literally, and is marked with a great mistrust and lack of
confidence in the policies of the Western Powers in the Near
East, leading even to hostility and open revolts against those policies. Arab opposition was now directed against the Western
"liberators" of the Near East and not towards the Turks whose
Empire had ceased to exist. Western political and economic
rivalries in this area helped further to aggravate the situation.

Since the second World War and particularly during the last
few years, a complex process of secularization is ushering in a
fourth stage in the evolution of Arab nationalism. This secularism
has its roots in various regional, territorial nationalisms, in the
adoption of the socio-economic principles of socialism and, to
a cerain extent, in the weakening of the ties of religion.
While the ideal of Arab unity is maintained, the political independence and sovereignty of the various Arab countries with all
their administrative regalia and state machinery have inevitably
accentuated and consolidated regional nationalisms. There is, for
instance, an Iraqi nationality distinct from a Syrian nationality.
And both are different from Lebanese nationality. The distinctness
and particularism of the various Arab nationalities may in the
long run be a negation of the dream of the universalists.

During this period, the Arab national movement has come
to be considered by many of its adherents as a shield and protection against Western imperialism and Western influences of
all kinds, and as a rallying point of Arab unification. It has become essentially a movement of emancipation—political, social and
even religious emancipation—from the political interference of
Western Powers, whether visible or invisible, from the feudal
spirit and mentality of the indigenous society and from the religious bond which has been the determinant factor in all political
concepts in Muslim countries. It also serves as a rallying point of
Arab unification: its appeal is to Pan-Arabism, reminding one of
the Pan-Slavic and Pan-Germanic movements of the nineteenth
century. Meanwhile, the "socialization" of Arab nationalism at

this stage seems to be an inevitable historical process through which the Near East is passing today, partly because of the suspicion and lack of confidence in Western democracy which hitherto has been represented in the Middle East by West European imperialism, partly because this is the only way at present in which secularism can invade the fortress of Islam, for socialism (and particularly Communism) combine "religious fervour" with a support for political emancipation which is entirely secular in spirit and application, and, finally, because of the awakening of the masses—of their desire to have the opportunity to "live the good life" and their rebellion against the old accepted notion that such an opportunity is the privilege of a minority and not the birth right of every human being.

Advocates of secular, socialized Arab nationalism base their concept of nationalism on the "Community (the *Umma)* feeling" of the Arabs and their "natural cohesion" as Arabs. They emphasize the "humanistic" aspect of such a nationalism which aims primarily at raising the social and economic standards of the workers and the peasants and at creating a new "Arab personality", freed from his social and religious past, emancipated politically and militarily from the West and united with his fellow Arabs in all Arab lands.

The trend towards an alliance between Arab nationalism and socialism seems to be receiving its greatest support from the educated youth and the urban masses in general. In every national crisis in recent years, this trend has been strengthened with the inevitable result that the Left has taken advantage of it and has, consequently, tried to assert itself as the custodian of Arab national interests. The national feeling has become, in turn, more vigorous, and ruthless, making it rapidly very difficult for any government to form a national policy without the support of the "nationalism of the masses".

It must not be assumed from the above classification that any clear or definite lines can be drawn between the various stages of Arab nationalism. There is a great deal of overlapping. The exponents of secular nationalism are still confined to a small class. Religion continues to be the dominating factor. A Muslim polity provides, at present, a higher potential of unity than any of the political divisions into which the Arab Near East has been split. Indeed, Arab nationalism, today, defies any definition—for no single definition can include all its divers and apparently contradictory aspects. Arab nationalism is both a political movement and a religious revival; it is both secular and theocratic; both a positive, constructive force aiming at the ideal of uniting all the Arab countries and a negative, uncompromising attitude towards the West. Much of the present uncertainty and confusion in thinking could be removed if there were a consensus of agreement in the Arab world on one definition of Arab nationalism and on one common goal for all the Arab countries.

It must be remembered, however, that Arab political nationalism is still in the early stages of its development. Political nationalism in the West was part of the process of the secularization of Christian civilization—a secularization which had, at least, some of its roots in the great cultural revolution known as the Renaissance. In the struggle between this nationalism and Christianity, the former won the day. It was a new god raised on the pagan altar of the State by men who thought they could find their salvation in a rational, man-made, social and political order. In the Arab East, in the nineteenth century, Islam was still too deeply rooted to be shaken by the nationalist ideas of the West and until the first quarter of the twentieth century, successfully resisted any attempt at secularization. The few Christians, and still fewer Muslims, who dreamt of establishing an Arab State on territorial, secular lines, as distinct from a Muslim State based on the theocratic, religious principles of the Qur'an, could not get any support from the vast majority of the inhabitants of these lands. Hence, Islam and Arab nationalism could not be divorced from each other. Thus, the new political nationalism was not the result of spiritual conflicts and tensions within the Muslim-Arab culture of the Muslim Arabs themselves. There has never been a Renaissance or a Reformation in Arab lands, in the European sense of those two terms.

Goethe once said that "he who would lift a great weight must find its center". Will the center of gravity of a renewed, rejuvenated and united Arab society be Islam or will it be a secular and socialized nationalism, if Islam finally fails to adapt itself to changing social and economic conditions in an evolving society? It remains to be seen whether an entirely secularized nationalism based on territory and territorial allegiance and loyalty is a possibility in Muslim lands.—i.e. whether political and social institutions could be divorced from religion. Such a concept of government, of political and social life has been, until now, incompatible with Islam as it has been, indeed, incompatible with any theocratic society, be it in the East or in the West. No amount of logical argument or of clever analogy with the rise of nationalism in Western Europe, can indicate in which direction Arab nationalism will finally develop. To what extent will Islam be able to adjust itself successfully to all secular and material forces which have invaded its lands in a thousand and one different forms, technological, political and social, is the key question of all the questions asked today about the Arab Near East.

Hence, the crisis of the Near East is essentially a spiritual crisis, the same crisis, in its fundamentals, as that which Christianity had to face in the sixteenth and seventeenth centuries and which led to the rise of the European State-systems and the destruction of the unity of the Medieval Church. All human crises are, in the last analysis, spiritual in essence, if we believe in the existence of a spiritual order to which man should belong. It is the contention of the author that the major conflicts between the East and the West and indeed within the East and the West are of a spiritual nature. No political or economic panaceas exist to provide a solution for the basic problems of the Near East, if such a solution be divorced from the moral law and from spiritual vision. It is one of the tragedies of the present situation that so few have been able to grasp this fundamental truth.

NOTES
AND REFERENCES

1. Chirol, Sir Valentine and others, *Reawakening of the Orient and other Essays,* (Yale, 1925), p. 3.

2. Sura 9, *Al-Tawbah:* "Repentance", v. 128.

3. Sura 3, *Al-'Imran* ("The Family of 'Imran"), v. 106.

4. Sura 21, *Al-Anbia'* ("The Prophets"), v. 91.

5. Zaidan, Jurji, *Ta'rikh al-Tamaddun al-Islami,* translated by D.S. Margoliouth under the title of Umayyads and Abbasids, (Gibb Memorial Series, vol. IV, London, 1907) pp. 71-72.

6. An Oriental Student, *The Modern Syrians,* p. 202.

7. See King 'Abdullah's *Muthakkarati,* p. 121 and *Al-Manar,* vol. XVI, Part 10, pp. 735-754.

8. D. H. Miller, *My Diary at the Peace Conference of Paris, 1918-1919* (New York, 1924) vol. IV, Document 250, pp. 297-299.

9. *Ibid.,* Document 251, p. 300.

APPENDIX A

THE OTTOMAN EMPIRE
AREA, POPULATION, RACES, RELIGIONS IN 1844[1]

The total area of the empire, including the tributary provinces, is estimated at 1,836,478 square miles, and the extent and population of the several grand divisions in Europe, Asia, and Africa are as follows:—

Divisions	Area sq. m.	Population	Pop/sq.m.
Turkey in Europe	203,628	15,500,000	76.1
Turkey in Asia	673,746	16,050,000	23.8
Turkey in Africa	959,104	3,800,000	3.9
Total	1,836,478	35,350,000	19.2

POPULATION

The total population, estimated according to the census taken in 1844 at 35,350,000, is distributed as follows, in the different divisions of the empire:—

Turkey in Europe

Thrace	1,800,000
Bulgaria	3,000,000
Roumelia and Thessaly	2,700,000
Albania	1,200,000
Bosnia and the Hersegovina	1,100,000
The Islands	700,000
Moldavia	1,400,000
Wallachia	2,600,000
Serbia	1,000,000

15,500,000

1. Farley, J. Lewis, *The Resources of Turkey*, pp. 2, 3.

TURKEY IN ASIA

Asia Minor, or Anatolia	10,700,000
Syria, Mesopotamia, and Kurdistan	4,450,000
Arabian	900,000

	16,050,000

TURKEY IN AFRICA

Egypt	2,000,000
Tripoli, Fez, and Tunis	1,800,000

	3,800,000

Total	35,350,000

RACES

The various races of which the population is composed may be thus classified:—

Races	In Europe	In Asia	In Africa	Total
Ottomans	2,100,000	10,700,000	....	12,800,000
Greeks	1,000,000	1,000,000	....	2,000,000
Armenians	400,000	2,000,000	....	2,400,000
Jews	70,000	80,000	....	150,000
Slavs or Slavonians	6,200,000	....	....	6,200,000
Roumains	4,000,000	....	....	4,000,000
Albanians	1,500,000	....	....	1,500,000
Tartars	16,000	20,000	....	36,000
Arabs	....	885,000	3,800,000	4,685,000
Syrians and Chaldeans	....	200,000	....	200,000
Druses	....	80,000	....	80,000
Kurds	....	1,000,000	....	1,000,000
Turkomans	....	85,000	....	85,000
Gipsies	214,000	....	....	214,000
Total	15,500,000	16,050,000	3,800,000	35,350,000

APPENDIX A 133

RELIGIONS

The classification according to religions is as follows:—

Religion	In Europe	In Asia	In Africa	Total
Greeks and Armenians	4,550,000	12,650,000	3,800,000	21,000,000
Mussulmans	10,000,000	3,000,000	....	13,000,000
Catholics[1]	640,000	260,000	....	900,000
Jews	70,000	80,000	....	150,000
Other sects	240,000	60,000	....	300,000
Total	15,500,000	16,050,000	3,800,000	35,350,000

1. Including Maronites (with a Patriarch at Kanobin
in Mount Lebanon) 140,000

APPENDIX B

THE OTTOMAN EMPIRE IN 1914
AREA AND POPULATION[1]

Summary:

	Area sq. miles	Population
Turkey in Europe	10,882	1,891,000
Turkey in Asia Minor, including Armenia and Kurdistan	271,262	12,657,800

The Arab Provinces in the Near East:

Mesopotamia

	Area sq. miles	Population
Mosul	35,130	500,000
Baghdad	54,540	900,000
Basra	53,580	600,000
Total	143,250	2,000,000

Syria

	Area sq. miles	Population
Aleppo	33,430	1,500,000
Zor (Independent sanjak)	30,110	100,000
Syria	37,020	1,000,000
Beirut	6,180	533,500
Jerusalem (Independent sanjak) ..	6,600	341,600
Lebanon	1,190	200,000
Total	114,530	3,675,100

1. Mears, E. G., *Modern Turkey*, pp. 580-581, citing *Stateman's Year-book*, 1921 Edition.

APPENDIX C

RESOLUTION VOTEES PAR LE CONGRES ARABE

« Le Congrès arabe, réuni à Paris, 184, Boulevard Saint-Germain, a adopté dans sa séance du 21 Juin 1913 les résolutions suivantes :

1. Des réformes radicales et urgentes sont nécessaires dans l'Empire Ottoman.

2. Il importe d'assurer aux arabes ottomans l'exercice de leurs droits politiques en rendant effective leur participation à l'administration centrale de l'Empire.

3. Il importe d'établir dans chacun des vilayets syriens et arabes un régime décentralisateur approprié à ses besoins et à ses aptitudes.

4. Le vilayet de Beyrouth, ayant formulé ses revendications dans un projet spécial voté le 31 Janvier 1913 par une Assemblé générale ad hoc est basé sur le double principe de l'extension des pouvoirs du conseil général du vilayet et de la nomination de conseillers étrangers, le Congrès demande la mise en application du susdit projet.

5. La langue arabe doit être reconnue au Parlement Ottoman et considérée comme officielle dans les pays syriens et arabes.

6. Le service militaire sera régional dans les vilayets syriens et arabes, en dehors des cas d'extrême nécessité.

7. Le Congrès émet le vœu de voir le Gouvernement Impérial Ottoman assurer au Liban les moyens d'améliorer sa situation financière.

8. Le Congrès affirme sa sympathie pour les demandes réformistes des arméniens ottomans.

9. Les présentes résolutions seront communiquées au Gouvernement Impérial Ottoman.

10. Il sera fait également communication des mêmes résolutions aux Puissances amies de l'Empire Ottoman.

11. Le Congrès exprime ses chaleureux remerciements au Gouvernement de la République pour sa généreuse hospitalité.

ANNEXE AUX PRECEDENTES RESOLUTIONS

« 1. Aussi longtemps que les résolutions votées par le présent Congrès n'auront pas été dûment exécutées, les membres des comités réformistes Arabes Syriens s'abstiendront d'accepter toute fonction dans l'Empire

Ottoman, à moins d'une autorisation expresse et spéciale de leurs comités respectifs.

2. Les présentes résolutions constitueront le programme politique des syriens et arabes ottomans. Aucun candidat aux élections législatives ne sera appuyé s'il ne s'est engagé au préalable à défendre le susdit programme et a en poursuivre l'exécution.

3. Le Congrès remercie les émigrés arabes de leur patriotisme et du concours qu'ils lui ont prêté, et leur transmet ses salutations par les soins de leurs délégués. »[1]

---

1. See Al-Lujnat al-'Ulya Li-Hizb al-Lamarkaziyah, *Al-Mu'tamar al-'Arabi al-Awwal*, pp. 132-134.

APPENDIX D

A PROGRAM OF REFORMS BASED ON
ADMINISTRATIVE DECENTRALIZATION

« Une grosse question commence à se poser : la question arabe. Toutes les personnes en contact avec les milieux arabes la prévoyaient depuis longtemps. Dès le mois de novembre dernier une personalité syrienne et musulmane, qui exerce en Syrie une grande influence et qui est remarquable par son intelligence et sa connaissance des choses de l'Europe, me disait :

'Aucun sentiment séparatiste n'existe chez nous. Nous tenons au contraire essentiellement à faire partie de l'Empire Ottoman, afin qu'un bloc solide, capable de resister aux appetits possibles de l'Europe, soit constitué. Mais nous considérons comme une condition *sine qua non* de notre loyalisme que le gouvernement ottoman nous accorde un régime administratif acceptable.'

« Successivement les conseils des vilayets de Beyrouth, d'Alep, de Tripoli, de Syrie, viennent de faire l'exposé de ce régime réclamé par les Arabes. Il s'agit d'une décentralisation poussée à l'extrême, confinant à l'autonomie. Les principaux points réclamés sont en effet :

« 1e. La reconnaissance de la langue arabe comme langue officielle de la province dans tous les bureaux et tribunaux, la langue turque restant langue officielle pour la correspondance avec Stamboul.

« Dans le projet rédigé par le Conseil du vilayet de Beyrouth, on demande même que l'usage de la langue arabe soit admis à la Chambre des Députés et au Sénat.

« 2e. Comme corollaire, seront nommés en Syrie des fonctionnaires connaissant la langue arabe. Provisoirement, une exception pour les valis ; elle prendra fin au bout d'une période de six ans, à dater de la promulgation de la loi ;

« 3e. Les autorités locales seront consultées pour nommer les fonctionnaires civils et judiciaires, les officiers de la gendarmerie ;

« 4e. Une haute cour sera instituée pour juger en cassation les jugements rendus dans les provinces de Jérusalem, Damas, Beyrouth et Alep etc. Actuellement, toute cassation se fait à Constantinople ;

« 5e. En temps de paix, le service militaire sera régional.

« 6e. Les revenus provinciaux seront divisés en deux catégories :

(a) Revenus des douanes, de postes et télégraphes et des impots militaires, à la disposition du gouvernement central ;

(b) Toutes autres recettes à la disposition du gouvernement local, pour être appliquées aux besoins de la province.

« 7e. Des conseils de vilayet seront créés ; ils auront des pouvoirs administratifs et, dans une certaine mesure, des pouvoirs législatifs étendus ;

« Toutes les questions, autres que celles de politique générale et de défense nationale abandonnées au gouvernement central, seront de leur compétence ;

« 8e. Des conseillers étrangers seront nommés pour réorganiser la gendarmerie, la police, la justice, les finances. Ils seront nommés pour quinze ans et choisis parmi les spécialistes europééns connaissant les usages locaux, la langue arabe ou turque.

« Certaines personnalités arabes m'ont déclaré dans leurs conversations qu'à titre de garantie elles désiraient quelque chose de plus encore : la présence d'un nombre minimum d'Arabes au conseil des ministres.

« Ces mêmes personnalités, aux quelles j'ai demandé si elles ne croyaient pas que le gouvernement central trouverait ces demandes bien radicales, m'ont répondu :

« 'Nous considérons ces demandes comme la simple application aux provinces Arabes des concessions faites aux Malissores, au printemps de 1911, et ensuite aux Albanais en général, durant l'été de 1912'.

« Le gouvernement de Ghazy Moukhtar Pacha a déclaré que ces réformes seraient étendues à toutes les populations de l'Empire. Le présent gouvernement se prêtera-t-il à ces demandes ? »[1]

---

1.   "L'Echo de Paris" of February 24, 1913, which in turn had reproduced this article from the "Daily Telegraph" of the previous day— cited in Contenson, Ludovic de, *Les Réformes en Turqie d'Asie. La Question Arménienne et la Question Syrienne*. pp. 63-67.

APPENDIX E

EXTRACT FROM THE ANNUAL REPORT
ON TURKEY FOR THE YEAR 1908

(Enclosure in Despatch from Sir G. Lowther
to Sir Edward Grey, No. 105 of February 17, 1909)

The Constitutional Movement

"For some years past, in and out of Turkey, it was generally known that a revolutionary movement set on foot by Young Turks was proceeding, but it was also generally thought that, thanks to the very complete system of espionage established by the Sultan, the development of the idea was surrounded by almost insuparable difficulties...

A Council of Ministers was called on the 23rd July. There were but two alternatives—to surrender to the demand, or to fight the rebels. It must have indeed appeared incomprehensible to His Majesty that, with the immense army he had always maintained, a handful of rebels could not be suppressed. But the Ministers realized that things had gone too far to turn back, and on the suggestion of Said Pasha they declared that their advice to the Sultan must be to grant the Constitution...

On the 31st July at the Selamlik in the presence of all the foreign Representatives the Sultan declared his firm resolve to uphold the Constitution, and a favourable impression was generally made by the freedom allowed to the people in the neighbourhood of the Palace to approach within the immediate proximity of the Sultan.

The early stages of the revolution were distinguished by a remarkable community of enthusiasm on the part of all races and religions throughout the Empire. It was impossible to view, without some scepticism, the picture of Greek and Moslem embracing one another and Moslem and Armenians flaunting their affection for one another. But after the first doubts that were felt in the more remote districts as to whether the movement was sincere, and whether it was not some trick on the part of the Sultan, had passed away, the sense of relief from the autocratic rule of the last thirty years became evident in every corner of the Empire...

In the meantime, the idea of the Constitution was being gradually assimilated throughout the country. Amongst the Arabs it produced but little impression, they seemed sceptical of reform, tolerating Turkish rule as a Moslem rule, and harbouring some veneration for the Sultan as the religious head of the Ottoman Empire. There were whispers of reaction, but in most cases it could be explained by the hesitation of those, who were not convinced of the future success of the movement, declining to throw themselves into the movement with enthusiasm...

It was at the end of October that the first tendency towards reaction made itself sufficiently felt to require notice in despatches. The Arabs wondered how far the Constitution was in accordance with the principles of Holy Law. The apathy of the Syrians towards the Constitution was complained of by the members of the League..."[1]

1.   Gooch, G. P. and Temperley, Harold (Edit.), *British Documents on the Origins of the War, 1898-1914*. Vol. V: *The Near East,* 1903-9 (London, 1928), pp. 249-258.

APPENDIX F

THE GENEALOGY OF THE OTTOMAN SULTANS

		Date of accession
1.	Uthman ("Osman")	1299
2.	Orkhan	1326
3.	Murad I	1360
4.	Bayezid I	1389
	(Interregnum—struggle for the Sultanate by Bayezid's three sons: Sulaiman, Muhammad and Musa)	1402-1413
5.	Muhammad I	1413
6.	Murad II	1421
7.	Muhammad II	1451
8.	Bayezid II	1481
9.	Selim I	1512
10.	Sulaiman I ("The Magnificent")	1520
11.	Selim II	1566
12.	Murad III	1574
13.	Muhammad III	1595

THE GENEALOGY OF THE OTTOMAN SULTANS (CONT'ED.)

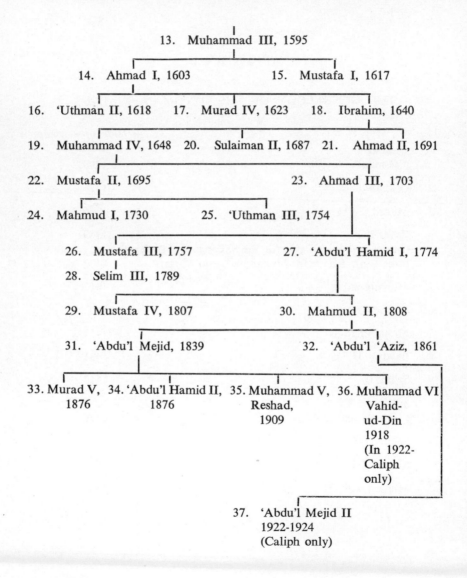

13. Muhammad III, 1595

14. Ahmad I, 1603   15. Mustafa I, 1617

16. 'Uthman II, 1618   17. Murad IV, 1623   18. Ibrahim, 1640

19. Muhammad IV, 1648   20. Sulaiman II, 1687   21. Ahmad II, 1691

22. Mustafa II, 1695   23. Ahmad III, 1703

24. Mahmud I, 1730   25. 'Uthman III, 1754

26. Mustafa III, 1757   27. 'Abdu'l Hamid I, 1774

28. Selim III, 1789

29. Mustafa IV, 1807   30. Mahmud II, 1808

31. 'Abdu'l Mejid, 1839   32. 'Abdu'l 'Aziz, 1861

33. Murad V, 34. 'Abdu'l Hamid II, 35. Muhammad V, 36. Muhammad VI
    1876   1876   Reshad,   Vahid-
                                         1909   ud-Din
                                                          1918
                                                          (In 1922-
                                                          Caliph
                                                          only)

37. 'Abdu'l Mejid II
     1922-1924
     (Caliph only)

It is to be noted that with the exception of three Sultans (Orkhan and Bayezid I and II), all the other Sultans' names are in Arabic.

BIBLIOGRAPHY

A SELECTED LIST OF REFERENCES

A. *(In English)*

Adams, Charles C.,
Islam and Modernism in Egypt
(London, 1933).

Antonius, George,
The Arab Awakening
(London, 1938 ... 1945).

Bailey, Frank Edgar,
British Policy and the Turkish Reform Movement—1826-1853
(Harvard University Press, 1942).

Barker, Edward B. B.,
Syria and Egypt under the Last Five Sultans of Turkey
2 Vols. (London, 1876).

Bell, Gertrude L.
Amurath to Amurath
(London, 1911).

Bell, Gertrude L.
The Desert and the Sown
(London, 1907).

Brocklemann, Carl,
History of Islamic Peoples
(English Ed. London, 1949),
(New York, 1947).

Chirol, Sir Valentine,
Fifty Years in a Changing World
(London, 1927).

Churchill, (Colonel)
Charles Henry,
The Druzes and the Maronites Under the Turkish Rule from 1840-1860
(London, 1862).

Cumming, Henry H.,
Franco-British Rivalry in the Post-War Near East
(London, 1938).

David, Wade Dewood,
European Diplomacy in the Near Eastern Question, 1906-1909
(Urbana, 1940).

Djemal Pasha — *Memoires of a Turkish Statesman 1913-1919* (London, n.d.).

Dodwell, Henry, — *The Founder of Modern Egypt. A Study of Mohammed Ali* (Cambridge, 1931).

Emin, Ahmed — *Turkey in the World War* (New Haven, 1930).

Farley, J. Lewis, — *Modern Turkey* (London, 1872).

Farley, J. Lewis, — *Turks and Christians* (London, 1876).

Farley, J. Lewis, — *The Resources of Turkey* Considered with Special Reference to the Profitable Investment and Capital in the Ottoman Empire (London, 1863).

Gibb, H. A. R., — *Modern Trends in Islam* (Chicago, 1947).

Gibb, H. A. R. and Bowen, Harold, — *Islamic Society and the West,* Vol. 1 (London, 1950).

Gooch, G. P. and Temperley, Harold (Edit.) — *British Documents on the Origins of the War, 1898-1914.* Vol. V: *The Near East, 1903-9* (London, 1928) and Vol. X: Part I. *The Near and Middle East on the Eve of the War* (London, 1936).

Goodell, Rev. William, (Prime, E. D. G. Edit.) — *Forty Years in the Turkish Empire* (New York, 1876).

Graves, Sir R. W., — *Storm Centres of the Near East 1879-1929* (London, 1933).

Great Britain, Admiralty, Geographical Section of the Naval Intelligence Division, — *A Handbook of Syria* (Including Palestine) (London, n.d.).

Great Britain, Admiralty, — *A Manual on the Turanians and Pan-Turanianism* (London, n.d.).

Great Britain, Foreign Office,   *Correspondence Relating to the*
                                  Affairs of Syria, 1860-61
                                  (London, 1861).

Great Britain, Foreign   *The Rise of Islam and the Caliphate*
   Office, Handbooks   (And) *The Pan-Islamic Movement*
   Prepared Under the   (London, January, 1919).
   Direction of the
   Historical Section of
   the Foreign Office:
   No. 96a & b,

   No. 96c & d,   *The Rise of the Turks* (And)
                                  The Pan-Turanian Movement
                                  (London, February 1919).

   No. 88,   *Turkey in Asia*
                                  (London, March 1919).

Heyd, Uriel,   *Foundations of Turkish Nationalism*
                                  (London, 1950).

Herbert, Audrey,   *Ben Kendim—A Record of Eastern*
                                  Travel
                                  (London, 1924).

Hourani, A. H.,   *Syria and Lebanon*
                                  (London, 1946).

Hourani, A. H.,   *Minorities in the Arab World*
                                  (London, 1947).

Howard, Harry N.,   *The Partition of Turkey—A*
                                  Diplomatic History 1913-1923
                                  (Norman, University of Oklahoma
                                  Press, 1931).

Ireland, Philip W. (Edit.)   *The Near East—Problems and*
                                  Prospects
                                  (University of Chicago Press,
                                  1942 ... 1945).

Jessup, H. H.,   *Fifty-Three Years in Syria*
                                  (New York, 1910).

Kirk, George, E.,   *A Short History of the Middle East*
                                  (London, 1952).

Knight, E. F.,   *The Awakening of Turkey*. A History
                                  of the Turkish Revolution.
                                  (London, 1909).

Kohn, Hans,	*A History of Nationalism in the East* (London, 1929).
Lawrence, T. E.,	*Seven Pillars of Wisdom* (Oxford, 1925).
Longrigg, H. S.,	*Four Centuries of Modern Iraq* (Oxford, 1925).
Longrigg, H. S.,	*Iraq, 1900 to 1950*. A Political, Social, and Economic History. (London, 1953).
Lybyer, A. H.,	*The Government of the Ottoman Empire in the time of Suleiman the Magnificent* (Harvard University Press, 1913).
Madden, Richard Robert,	*The Turkish Empire in its Relations with Christianity and Civilization* (London, 1862).
Mears, E. G.,	*Modern Turkey* (New York, 1924).
Midhat Bey, Ali Haydar,	*The Life of Midhat Pasha* (London, 1903).
Miller, William,	*The Ottoman Empire and its Successors, 1801-1922* (Cambridge, 1923).
Napier, Lieut.-Col., E.,	*Reminiscences of Syria and the Holy Land* 2 Vols. (London, 1847).
Pears, Sir Edwin,	*Life of 'Abdu'l-Hamid* (New York, 1917).
Pears, Sir Edwin,	*Forty Years in Constantinople, 1873-1915* (New York, 1916).
Porter, J.,	*Five Years in Damascus* (London, 1870)
Ramsaur, Jr., E. E.,	*The Young Turks—Prelude to the Revolution of 1908* (Princeton, 1957).
Stitt, George,	*A Prince of Arabia: the Emir Shereef 'Ali Haider* (London, 1948).

Stoddard, Lothrop,   *The New World of Islam*
(New York, 1922).

Stripling, G. W. F.,   *The Ottoman Turks and the Arabs*
(Urbana, University of Illinois Press,
1942).

Susa, Nasim,   *The Capitulary Regime of Turkey,
Its History, Origin and Nature*
(Baltimore, 1933).

Temperley, H. W. V., (Ed.)   *The History of the Peace Conference
of Paris,* Vol. VI
(London, 1924).

Urquhart, David,   *The Lebanon (Mount Souria)*
A History and a Diary
(London, 1860).

Urquhart, David,   *The Spirit of the East,* 2 Vols.
(London, 1839).

Wortabet, Gregory M.,   *Syria and the Syrians, or Turkey In
the Dependencies* 2 Vols.
(London, 1856).

Young, George,   *Nationalism and War in the Near
East*
(Oxford, 1915).

ANONYMOUS :

An Oriental Student,   *The Modern Syrians*
(London, 1844).

A Diplomatist,   *Nationalism and War in the Near
East*
(Oxford, 1915).

A German Diplomat,   *The Near East from Within*
(London, 1915).

B. *(In French)*

Aboussouan, Benoît,	*Le Problème Politique Syrien* (Paris, 1925).
Arminjon, Pierre,	*De la Nationalité dans l'Empire Ottoman* (Paris, 1903).
Azoury, Negib,	*Le Réveil de la Nation Arabe dans l'Asie Turque* (Paris, 1905).
Brémond, Général Ed.,	*Le Hedjaz dans la Guerre Mondiale* (Paris, 1931).
Contenson, Baron Ludovis de,	*Les Réformes en Turquie d'Asie La Question Arménienne, La Question Syrienne* (Paris, 1913).
Cuinet, Vital,	*Syrie, Liban et Palestine* Paris, 1896).
Engelhardt, Ed.,	*La Turquie et le Tanzimat* (Paris, 1882).
France, Ministère des Affaires Etrangères,	*Documents Diplomatiques 1860* (Paris, 1861).
France,	*Archives du Ministère des Affaires Etrangères — Turquie* (19ème siècle).
Freycinet, C. de,	*La Question d'Egypte* (Paris, n.d.).
Gaulis, B. G.,	*La Question Arabe* (Paris, 1930).
Gouilly, Alphonse,	*L'Islam devant le Monde Moderne* (Paris, 1904).
Guys, M. Henry,	*Esquisse de l'Etat Politique et Commercial de la Syrie* (Paris, 1862).
Jouplain, M.,	*La Question du Liban* (Paris, 1908).
Jung, Eugène,	*La Révolte Arabe* (Paris, 1924).

Jung, Eugène,   *Les Puissances devant la Révolte Arabe* (Paris, 1906).

Khairallah, K. T.,   *Les Régions Arabes Libérées* (Paris, 1919).

Mandelstam, André,   *Le sort de l'Empire Ottoman* (Paris, 1917).

Montagne, R.,   *L'Evolution Moderne des Pays Arabes* (Paris, 1935).

Nerval, Gérard de,   *Voyage en Orient, 1851* (Paris, 1927).

Pichon, Jean,   *Le Partage du Proche Orient* (Paris, 1938).

Rivoyre, Denis, de   *Les Vrais Arabes et leur Pays* (Paris, 1884).

Saba, Jean S.,   *L'Islam et la Nationalité* (Paris, 1931).

Samné, Georges,   *La Syrie* (Paris, 1920).

Young, George, Edit.   *Corps de Droit Ottoman* 7 vols. (Oxford, 1905).

C. *(In Arabic)*

'Abdu, Shaikh Muhammad, and al-Afghani, Jamal-ad-Din,   *Al-'Urwat al-Wuthka La Inqisama Laha* (Cairo, 1328 A.H.).

Al-'Alami, Shaikh 'Abdullah,   *A'zam Tithkar l'il 'Uthmaniyin al-Ahrar, aw al-Hurriyah wa'l Musawat wa'l Mab'uthan* (Beirut, 1326, A.H.).

Al-A'zami, Ahmad 'Izzat,   *Al-Qadiyah al-'Arabiyah* (Baghdad, 1931).

Al-'Azm, 'Uthman (Edit.,),   *Majmu'at Athar Rafiq Bey Al-'Azm* (Cairo, 1344 A.H.).

150　　　　　　　　　　BIBLIOGRAPHY

'Aziz Bey, *Suriya wa Lubnan fi'l Harb al-'Alamiyah* (Translated from Turkish by Fuad Maydani. Beirut, 1933).

Al-Bustani, Sulaiman, *Al-Dawlah al-'Uthmaniyah Qabl al-Dustur wa Ba'dahu* (Beirut, 1908).

Al-Dimishqi, Mikha'il, *Ta'rikh Hawadith al-Sham wa Lubnan* (Beirut, 1912).

Halim, Ibrahim Bey, *Kitab al-Tu'hfa al-Halimiyah fi Tarikh al-Dawlah al-'aliyah* (Cairo, 1905).

Hatatah, Yusuf Kamal, *Mudhakkarat Midhat Pasha* (Cairo, n.d.).

Ibn-Al-Husain, 'Abdullah (King) *Al-Amali al-Siyasiyah* ('Amman, 1939).

Ibn-Al-Husain, 'Abdullah (King) *Mudhakkarati* (Jerusalem, 1945).

Al-Kawakibi, 'Abd-al-Rahman, *Taba'i' al-Istibdad wa Masari' al-Isti'bad* (Cairo, n.d.).

Al-Khalidi, M. R., *Al-Inqilab al-'Uthmani wa Turkiya al-Fatat* (Cairo, 1326 A.H.).

Kurd-'Ali, Muhammad, *Khitat al-Sham,* vols. II, III, and V. (Damascus, 1925 and 1927).

Al-Lujnat al-'Ulya li-Hizb al-Lamarkaziyah, *Al-Mu'tamar al-'Arabi al-Awwal* Held in Paris, June 18th-23rd, 1913 (Cairo, 1913).

Al-Makhzumi, Muhammad, *Khatirat Jamal-al-Din al-Afghani al-Husaini* (Beirut, 1931).

Mas'ad, Bulos, *Al-Dawlat al-'Uthmaniyah fi Lubnan wa Suriyah, 1517-1916* (Cairo, 1916).

Mas'ad, Bulos, *Lubnan wa Suriyah Qabl al-Intidab wa Ba'dahu,* vol. I, (Cairo, 1929).

Niyazi, Ahmad,   *Khawatir Niyazi*
                                   (Cairo, 1909)—Translated from
                                   Turkish by Wali-al-Din Yakan.

Nusuli, Anis Zakariya,   *Asbab al-Nahdat al-'Arabiyah
                                   fi'l Qarn al-Tasi'-'ashar*
                                   (Beirut, 1926).

Al-Rihani, Amin,   *Muluk al-'Arab,* vol. II
                                   (Beirut, 1929).

Sarkis, Salim,   *Sirr Mamlakah*
                                   (Cairo, 1895).

ANONYMOUS:

                                   Thawrat al-'Arab
                                   (Cairo, 1916).

                                   Ma Hunalik
                                   (Cairo, 1896).